THE FORBIDDEN CITY

WONDERS OF THE WORLD

....

THE FORBIDDEN CITY

GEREMIE R. BARMÉ

Harvard University Press
Cambridge, Massachusetts
2008

First published in the United Kingdom in 2008 by
Profile Books Ltd
3A Exmouth House
Pine Street
Exmouth Market
London ECIR OJH
www.profilebooks.com

Printed in the United States of America

Library of Congress Cataloging-in-Publication Data

Barmé, Geremie.
    The Forbidden City / by Geremie R. Barmé
        p.   cm.—(Wonders of the World)
"First published in the United Kingdom by Profile Books ... London"—T.p.
Includes bibliographical references.
ISBN-13: 978-0-674-02779-4 (alk. paper)
ISBN-10: 0-674-02779-5 (alk. paper)
1. Forbidden City (Beijing, China)--History. I. Title.
DS795.8.F67B37 2007
951'.156—dc22   2007040893

For Jocelyn Chey
and in memory of
Hans Moon Lin Chey

CONTENTS

INTRODUCTION

In his 1917 story 'The Great Wall of China' Franz Kafka evokes the Forbidden City and the imperial Chinese court in the following way:

Around the emperor, the glittering and yet mysterious court throngs – malice and enmity clothed as servants and friends, the counterbalance to the imperial power, with their poisoned arrows always trying to shoot the emperor down from his side of the balance scales. The empire is immortal, but the individual emperor falls and collapses. Even entire dynasties finally sink down and breathe their one last death rattle. The people will never know anything about these struggles and sufferings.

This may be a fanciful description, an oriental fantasy, but it also echoes the views some twentieth-century Chinese had of their own country's dynastic past. Like the Great Wall of China, the Forbidden City has a metaphorical life, and it has provided an abiding alibi for misunderstandings.

Both the reality of an imperial court sequestered behind the vermilion walls of the Forbidden City in Beijing and the mysterious, but none the less powerful, perception of a secretive and hidden world at the heart of the enigma of China have contributed to the image of an inscrutable, capricious

and cruel regime. The Empress Dowager Cixi who dominated the Chinese court for nearly fifty years from the mid
nineteenth century personified the untold story of the Forbidden City. Tales of dark plots and savagery at the court of the
Empress Dowager would repel and intrigue people in China
and throughout the world. From her time, writers have been
beguiled by the architecture of imperial Beijing and quick
to employ the language of court politics to describe events
there. Not only that, but in many films, novels and plays, as
well as in journalistic accounts, both Western and Chinese,
there has been a tendency to conflate court secrecy, traditional
politics and the intricate design of the palaces with the nature
of the Chinese people and society as a whole. As Simone de
Beauvoir remarked, the 'city into which the population is not
admitted has obviously usurped the title of city'.

For twentieth-century Chinese writers, educators and
revolutionaries, the Forbidden City became emblematic of
the country's rigidity and backwardness; it housed the canker
of autocracy which they blamed for keeping China from
taking its rightful place alongside the other great nations of
the modern world. In many ways, however, the Forbidden
City and its modern fate parallel the history of modern China
itself. This book traces that history, as well as discusses those
who would penetrate the Forbidden City, literally or metaphorically. Using recent scholarship, it also travels back in
time to allow us to follow the daily routine of an emperor.
We also reconsider the controversial figure of the Empress
Dowager, among others, and engage in the debates that have
raged in modern China over what to do with the empty heart
of the dynastic past.

There are many ways of understanding the Forbidden

City. From the very beginning, it was designed to be a place of display and spectacle. In the 1410s, the Ming emperor Yongle (pronounced Yung-lerh, r. 1403–24) moved his court from Nanjing ('the southern capital') to Beijing ('the northern capital'), for which he designed a grand plan. The Forbidden City was built within a series of massive crenellated enclosures to create nothing less than a terrestrial refraction of the realm of the celestial Jade Emperor, or Heavenly Ancestor, and his court which was said to rule over the universe. Approached through imposing gates and enceintes – the Outer City, the Inner City – and along an Imperial Way flanked by the central ministries of the government of the empire and finally into the Imperial City through three more massive gates, the Forbidden City covered over 72 hectares containing imposing imperial structures and vast courtyards, as well as over 900 rooms. It was conceived on such a monumental scale so as to awe not only the subjects of China, but also the tributary peoples who lived along the extensive borders of Ming territory. It was also the focal point of imperial rites and festivals designed to ensure the harmony of heaven, earth and man.

As the art historian Simon Leys observed of the palace:

[T]his vast gathering of courts and palaces remains one of the most sublime architectural creations in the world. In the history of architecture, most monuments that try to express imperial majesty abandon the human scale and cannot reach their objective without reducing their occupants to ants. Here, on the contrary, greatness always keeps an easy measure, a natural scale; it is conveyed not by a disproportion between the monument and the onlooker but by an infallibly harmonious space. The just nobility of these courts and roofs, endlessly reaffirmed under the

changing light of different days and seasons, gives the onlooker
that physical feeling of happiness which only music can sometimes
convey. As a body loses weight in water, the visitor feels a light-
ening of his being to swim thus in such perfection …

The Forbidden City was, as the name suggests, a city unto itself. It contained grand ceremonial halls raised on high marble platforms in which the emperor and his ministers officiated over the day-to-day administration of the empire. These were located in what was called the Outer Court. Behind these and to the north of the formal throne rooms and offices of the bureaucracy was the Inner Court. This was strictly isolated from the more public areas of the Forbidden City. The Inner Court housed the imperial family and its army of retainers in numerous 'palaces', generally single-storey courtyard residences with large formal buildings and more intimate living areas. These lavish structures were allotted to the female members of the imperial family according to rank and intimacy with the throne. The palaces within the larger city palace of the Forbidden City were the setting for much of the drama of court life. The wealth of empire and the cloistered nature of absolute power allowed successive Ming rulers (1368–1644) to pursue their own pleasures within the Inner Court whenever they tired of the strictures of royal routine and the burdens of running a vast empire.

After years of increasingly corrupt rule, the Ming faltered. Rebel forces invaded the Celestial Capital in the 1640s, destroying much of the city itself. A Ming loyalist, hoping that an army led by Manchus from the north-east would help defeat the rebel chief occupying the dragon throne, allowed the Manchu military juggernaut to pass through the

Great Wall. The last Ming ruler, the Chongzhen Emperor (r. 1627–44) had already committed suicide on a hill immediately behind the palace. The Manchus did oust the rebels, but they also overthrew the Ming, bringing an end to Han Chinese rule. The Manchus, a non-Han 'foreign' race, established the capital of their 'invasion dynasty' of the Qing in Beijing. They were regarded by the people of the old Ming empire as conquering barbarians, but over the following centuries the Manchu rulers worked hard to show the supposedly more highly civilised Han people that they had the moral authority, as well as the cultural finesse, to rule over the vast Ming territory. They rebuilt Beijing on an even grander scale than before and dominated that city and an expanded Chinese empire until an anti-monarchist revolution forced them to abdicate 268 years later, in early 1912.

The Manchus had their own reservations about the design and pitfalls of the Forbidden City, which they found claustrophobic – perhaps not surprising for a people used to roaming immense territories of what is now north-east China. They spent long months every year at the garden palaces they built outside the walls of Beijing and far beyond the Great Wall at their extensive mountain lodge at Chengde and at the Mulan hunting grounds even further north. Some were outspokenly disturbed by the confining atmosphere of the imperial maze. In the mid nineteenth century, for example, the Empress Dowager's son, the Tongzhi Emperor, described the place in which he grew up as being like a warren of 'dank ditches with vermilion walls and green-tiled roofs'.

The first foreigners to enter the imperial demesne in the sixteenth century came to convert the court to Christianity; they were not successful. Traders, men who were willing to resort to force, and even war, to achieve their goals eventually followed. The accounts of these two groups, scholar missionaries and canny merchants, colour views of what was often known as the 'Great Within' and its occupants to the present day: to them the Forbidden City was a labyrinthine mystery ruled over by capricious oriental despots and their impotent courtiers.

The palace and its intrigues, its mystique and its history have thus played a central role in defining both Chinese and Western perceptions of China. In 1912, upon the fall of the Qing dynasty, the Republic of China was founded. Its first president, Yuan Shikai, established his offices in the Lake Palaces, the imperial pleasure gardens adjacent to the Forbidden City. The Republic enjoyed an unsteady rule beset by internecine strife, followed, in the 1930s and 1940s, by invasion and occupation by the Japanese. After a short-lived postwar peace a titanic struggle broke out between the Nationalist rulers of the Republic and Communist insurgents who had grown strong during the struggle with Japan and whose clean-living image offered a stark contrast to the rampant corruption of the old regime. Thirty-five years after the fall of the Qing dynasty, at the time of the creation of the People's Republic of China, Mao Zedong and his comrades also chose to locate their Communist government in the former imperial enclave of the Lake Palaces. This only reinforced the impression, however, that, while rulers may come and go, the system as well as the habits of Chinese autocracy stay the same. As Franz Kafka put it, 'the empire is immortal'. As much as Mao and his fellow revolutionaries might rail against the habits of the feudal past, their language, literary references and political infighting were carried out in its shadow. The palace, a metaphor for Old China, persisted as a metaphor for New China.

Mao and his comrades did not have a comfortable relationship with the Forbidden City, however, and they even considered demolishing it or converting it for other purposes. They were a revolutionary force far more radical than their Republican predecessors. They occupied Beijing and gradually displaced its original citizens. New Party activists worked hard to mobilise the expanded population to join in a mass campaign to refashion the ancient capital. Mao himself refused to enter the Forbidden City after 1949 but, inspired by the Soviet inhabitants of the Kremlin (and the advisers they sent to Beijing in the early 1950s), he and other Party leaders imagined moving into a modern 'Chairman's Office' built opposite the palace, a socialist edifice that would outstrip in scale and majesty the Hall of Supreme Harmony, the largest wooden building in China and the formal centre of dynastic power. In the late 1950s, when surveying the newly created expanse of Tiananmen Square (built on the former Imperial Way that led to the Forbidden City), Mao famously remarked that one day he hoped to look out on a vista of factory chimneys.

Today, the visitor who ascends the Gate of Heavenly Peace – the grand entrance to the Imperial City that features a rostrum built for Chinese Communist Party leaders to review mass parades – is lucky to see anything at all. Beijing's few smoke-belching factories were mostly relocated in the run up to the 2008 Olympics, but the smog haze of hyper-development still blankets and obscures the city for much of the year. The walls of old Beijing have long since been razed, as have most of the neighbourhoods that reflected the city's ancient temper. Yet for all of the destructive change that has been visited on the Chinese capital in the last sixty years, the Forbidden City remains. It is unique, the most tangible symbol of a Beijing that is no more.

In the twentieth century, the Forbidden City became a monument to the passage of dynastic China. Today, the Palace Museum that occupies much of the sprawling Forbidden City is one of the major tourist attractions of China's metropolitan capital. It showcases (albeit in museological rivalry with the lavish National Palace Museum in Taipei) the material heritage of the nation. It symbolises what, after a century of repudiation, is now regarded as being China's proud imperial past.

The English literary historian and essayist Peter Quennell visited the Forbidden City not long after it was first opened to the public in October 1925:

> *Something in the atmosphere of a palace or temple starts to putrefy when the human occupants vanish ...*
>
> Sic transit. *The tag slips out so easily; there was a time when the past glories of the world went up in smoke at the touch of change. Nowadays we are more conservative of fallen splendour and empty palaces, from Peking to Madrid, are handed over to a dim rabble of custodians who punch tickets, jingle coins and erect notice boards.*

For all of its vast expanse and grandeur the Forbidden City is a sombre and haunting presence.

A READER'S GUIDE

As a volume in the series Wonders of the World this book was not designed to be a conventional guide to the Forbidden City in Beijing. It is a book that has a particular architecture, one to which the reader might need a guide. It offers a non-chronological history of the Forbidden City from its creation in the 1410s, as well as an account of some of its inhabitants and the stories of their involvement with the late dynastic and modern history of China in which they played a part. While guiding the reader through the numerous courtyards, halls and palaces that make up the Forbidden City, and the Lake Palaces adjacent to it, the book describes the events that surround the imperial centre of China, be they in the distant or the recent past. Those events have also shaped international perceptions of China, and have been recycled by Chinese thinkers and polemicists in discussions of their own country throughout the twentieth century.

Navigating a course through the palace along the axes of both space and time, the book introduces the reader to the paradoxical relationship that has existed between the post-dynastic rulers of China – in the Republic of China (1912–1949), and during the first five and a half decades of the People's Republic of China (1949–) – and their constantly changing imperial legacy. The Forbidden City loomed large in China's twentieth century as the material centre of defunct dynastic rule and as a shade of inward-looking despotism. The rulers of modern China have actively worked to transform China into a strong and modern nation while in their various ways rejecting, affirming and falling prey to the autocratic attitudes and practices that found concrete expression in the Forbidden City.

Parenthetical updates are often included in or at the end of relevant paragraphs. They indicate how a particular area or feature has been transformed since the end of the last dynasty.

EMPERORS AND THEIR NAMES

In imperial China the founder of a dynasty would establish the rule of his clan and all future emperors were chosen from among his male descendants. Zhu Yuanzhang founded the Ming dynasty in 1368, and all subsequent Ming rulers were members of the Zhu family. The Qing dynasty (1644–1911) was established by the Aisin Gioro clan of Manchu people, that is non-Han 'foreigners' who came from the north-east of modern-day China, and the Qing emperors all belonged to the Aisin Gioro.

The period during which Zhu Yuanzhang ruled China (1368–98) was known as the Hongwu reign, or the 'abundantly martial' era. Such 'reign titles' were chosen after a laborious process of discussion and reference to classical sources. It was hoped that auspicious reign titles would reflect both the aspirations and the reality of the ruler's life. The great Qing emperor Aisin Gioro Hongli ruled under the reign title Qianlong ('enduring glory'), and he is most commonly known by that name. The translations of these titles, which are generally based on those of Herbert A. Giles, are merely approximations. A list of the emperors, empresses dowager, regents and pretenders to the throne mentioned in the text can be found at the end of the book.

A NOTE ON ROMANISATION

Official Standard Chinese Spelling (*Hanyu pinyin*) is used throughout.

C is pronounced 'ts'. Cixi was previously written Tz'u-hsi.

Q is pronounced 'tch'. Qianlong was previously written Ch'ien-lung.

X is pronounced 'shh' although more dental. Kangxi was previously written K'ang-hsi.

Z is pronounced 'dz'. Thus, *za* (smash) is pronounced 'dzaa'.

Zh is pronounced 'dzh'. Tongzhi was previously written T'ung-chih.

TIMELINE

1368: the Ming dynasty founded by Zhu Yuanzhang with its capital in Nanjing ('the southern capital'). The Mongol Yuan dynasty (1279–1368) city of Dadu ('the great capital') is renamed Beiping ('the north pacified').

1403: Zhu Di usurps the throne of the Ming dynasty, assumes the reign title of Yongle and, despite protests, in 1406 he orders the relocation of the dynastic capital from Nanjing to his powerbase in Beiping, which is renamed Beijing ('the northern capital').

1416–20: the major structures of what becomes known as the Forbidden City are built, although over the centuries frequent fires and reconstruction will see many buildings refashioned and renamed.

1542: 27 November, palace women make an attempt on the life of the Jiajing Emperor. Thereafter, he lives in the West Gardens adjacent to the Forbidden City.

1600–20: the Wanli Emperor refuses to appear at audiences or meet with his ministers for years on end instead lavishing attention on his tomb.

1644: Beijing is invaded by Li Zicheng, the Marauding Prince and his rebel troops. The last Ming Emperor commits suicide on the hill behind the Forbidden City. The Manchu armies are invited through the Great Wall to help rid Beijing of the rebels. They occupy the city and enthrone the Shunzhi Emperor, ruler of the Manchu Qing dynasty.

1684: the Kangxi Emperor, Shunzhi's son, undertakes his first imperial tour of the south.

1690: 16 January, the Jesuit Jean-François Gerbillon records the layout of the Hall of Mental Cultivation, the Manchu emperors' preferred residence in the Forbidden City.

1722: the Kangxi Emperor dies in his garden palace northwest of Beijing, and is succeeded by his son, who rules as the Yongzheng Emperor.

1735: the Yongzheng Emperor builds the Palace of Longevity and Health. He dies the same year and is succeeded by his son who becomes the Qianlong Emperor.

1763: Cao Xueqin, the author of *The Dream of the Red Chamber*, dies.

1765: 28 January, one day in the reign of the Qianlong Emperor.

1793: the Qianlong Emperor receives a diplomatic mission from the court of George III led by Lord Macartney.

1795: approaching his sixtieth year on the throne, the Qian-long Emperor declares that, not wishing to exceed the sixty-one year reign of his grandfather, the Kangxi Emperor, he will retire in favour of his son to live in his 'mini Forbidden City'. In reality, he rules until his death in 1799.

1813: during the reign of the Jiaqing Emperor, Qianlong's son, adherents of the rebellious Heavenly Principle religious sect infiltrate the Forbidden City.

1839–42: the First Opium War, also known as the first of the Anglo-Chinese Wars. China cedes Hong Kong to Queen Victoria.

1856–60: the Second Opium War results in the defeat of the Qing empire. In September 1860, an Anglo-French Expeditionary Force invades Beijing following failed negotiations over the concluding treaty. The imperial garden palaces north-west of the city created during the reigns of the three great Qing emperors are looted and razed. The reigning Xianfeng Emperor, who has fled to the Imperial Hunting Lodge at Chengde, dies the following year leading to the rise of the Empress Dowager Cixi. Along with her co-regent, the Empress Dowager Ci'an, they ruled from 'behind the screen' during the minority first of the Tongzhi Emperor, and then of the Guangxu Emperor.

1873: foreign diplomats are received in audience by the Tongzhi Emperor at the Hall of the Radiant Dawn in the Lake Palaces.

1884: as the Guangxu Emperor comes into his majority, the Empress Dowager formally retires to the Palace of Accumulated Elegance.

1898: after a 100-day period of reform, the Empress Dowager resumes direct control over the court.

1900: the Boxer Rebellion results in a siege of the Legation Quarter in Beijing. As foreign forces approach, the Empress Dowager flees the capital with the emperor to Xi'an, his favourite the Pearl Concubine having died in mysterious circumstances. In August, following the relief of the Legations and the crushing of the Boxers, soldiers of the Eight-Power Allied Expeditionary Force occupy the Forbidden City and loot it.

1905: J. O. P. Bland and Edmund T. Backhouse's *China under the Empress Dowager* is published to international acclaim.

1908: the Empress Dowager Cixi and the Guangxu Emperor die. Three-year-old Puyi is installed as the Xuantong Emperor.

1911: a rebellion in October leads to the collapse of the Qing dynasty. The Xuantong Emperor abdicates the throne the following year, bring an end to over two millennia of imperial rule. Puyi's 'little court' is restricted to the Inner Court of the Forbidden City.

1912: 10 October, the Republic of China is inaugurated.

1913: 10 October, Yuan Shikai is installed as the president of the Republic of China and establishes his government in the Lake Palaces. On this day the following year, the Gallery of Antiquities opens to select visitors in the Hall of Martial Valour in the Outer Court of the Forbidden City. The three halls are also opened to the public for the first time.

1915: Yuan Shikai proclaims himself to be the Hongxian Emperor and plans his enthronement in the Hall of Supreme Harmony the following year.

1917: July, Zhang Xun attempts to restore the Qing house. Puyi takes the throne in the Hall of Supreme Harmony under his reign title of Xuantong, leading to nationwide opposition. The Forbidden City is attacked by air, resulting in minimum damage. After 12 days on the throne, Puyi abdicates.

1922: Victor Segalen's novel *René Leys* is published.

1923: 27 June, the Palace of Established Happiness burns down in mysterious circumstances. The following day, the abdicated emperor Puyi evicts most of the remaining eunuchs from the Inner Court.

1924: 5 November, the last emperor and his 'little court' are expelled from the Forbidden City.

1925: 10 October, the newly established Palace Museum opens the Inner Court to the public. The restaurant Emulating the Imperial Table opens in North Sea Park.

1928: following the success of the Northern Expedition which defeats the warlords in north China and unifies the country the national government, with its capital in Nanjing, orders that the old imperial capital of Beijing revert to its early Ming dynasty name Beiping. Part of the Lake Palaces is opened to the public and, in 1933, a swimming pool is built there.

1931: the threat of Japanese invasion leads to the evacuation of Palace Museum treasures to the south, first to Nanjing and later to the war-time capital of Chongqing.

1934: Puyi is enthroned as the Kangde Emperor of the Japanese puppet regime of Manchukuo. He is detained following the surrender of Japan in 1945 and is eventually 'reformed' by the Communists to become a model citizen of new China.

1937: the Japanese occupy Beiping and establish their civilian government in the Lake Palaces.

1943: Edmund T. Backhouse completes his memoir, *Décadence Manchoue*.

1944: Guo Moruo publishes 'Commemoration of the Three-Hundredth Year since *Jiashen* [1644]' which is praised by Mao Zedong.

1948: despite a state of civil war existing between the Republican government under the Nationalists and the Communist Party, the Gallery of Antiquities and the Palace Museum are merged in the Forbidden City. As the civil war nears an end, the Nationalist authorities order key treasures in the Palace Museum collection evacuated to Taiwan.

1949: 1 October, the People's Republic of China is established, Beiping is renamed Beijing to become the capital of socialist China. The Lake Palaces of Zhongnan Hai become the site of the Party and civil administration of the new government.

1950: March, the first exhibition of the Central Museum of the Revolution is held in the Hall of Martial Valour, formerly the Gallery of Antiquities. Also in March, Mao and his colleagues view the film *The Secret History of the Qing Court* at a special screening in the Lake Palace. Subsequently, Mao orders a nationwide denunciation of the film. October, the first state funeral for a Communist Party leader is held at the Ancestral Temple. Mervyn Peake's novel *Gormenghast* is published.

1952: the ''49 Scheme' for the preservation of Beijing is rejected, followed the next year by the announcement of plans to demolish the city walls.

1956: May, the Upper Northern Gate, the northern entrance to the Forbidden City, is demolished.

1958: a massive expansion of Tiananmen Square is undertaken and Mao lets it be known that he wants Beijing totally transformed. Ten Great Edifices are built as part of the celebration of the first decade of the People's Republic. Mao praises the destruction of other walled cities and launches the

Great Leap Forward that lasts until 1960, with devastating consequences and incalculable loss of life.

1960: February, a ten-year plan for central Beijing is announced, including an east–west highway in front of the Meridian Gate.

1963: the film *55 Days at Peking* is released internationally.

1964: expansion of the east–west Chang'an Boulevard through the centre of Beijing.

1965: the National Palace Museum opens in the northern Taipei suburb of Shilin, Taiwan.

1966: May, a People's Liberation Army work team is sent to the Forbidden City to 'revolutionise' the Palace Museum. Red Guards put up the sign 'A Palace of Blood and Tears' at the north entrance of the Forbidden City. 16 August, Red Guards unsuccessfully attempt to storm the palace. 18 August, the first mass rally of Red Guards in Tiananmen Square is held to celebrate the Cultural Revolution. Premier Zhou Enlai dispatches a battalion of troops to occupy the palace.

1967: June, Red Guards hold a mass song and dance performance in the forecourt of the Meridian Gate to celebrate the twenty-fifth anniversary of the publication of Mao Zedong's *Talks at the Yan'an Forum on Literature and Art*.

1967–70: the Forbidden City is closed to the public.

1970: September, Zhou Enlai instructs staff of the Palace Museum to prepare to re-open the Forbidden City.

1971: Simon Leys' *The Chairman's New Clothes* is published. April, a US ping-pong team visits the Forbidden City. US President Richard Nixon visits the following year. 1 May, Mao Zedong's last public appearance, with Lin Biao, on the rebuilt Gate of Heavenly Peace.

1973: the contents of the Buddhist prayer hall of the Palace of Benevolent Tranquillity are removed to White Horse Temple in Henan province. The Screen Building is constructed on either side of West Flourishing Gate in the Forbidden City.

1976: January, Zhou Enlai dies; September, Mao Zedong dies; October, the 'Gang of Four' is arrested.

1977: September, the Mausoleum of Chairman Mao containing the dead leader's embalmed corpse is opened on the site of the former Great Qing Gate in Tiananmen Square.

1978: a Communist Party congress brings a formal end to the era of Maoist-style socialism and Cultural Revolution politics, and inaugurates policies aimed at economic growth.

1981: Sun Jingxuan publishes his poem 'A Spectre Prowls Our Land'.

1983: Li Han-hsiang's film *Ruling behind the Screen* is released.

1987: the ousted former Party General Secretary, Hu Yaobang, is 'cast into a cold palace' and succeeded by Zhao Ziyang.

1988: Bernardo Bertolucci's Oscar-winning film *The Last Emperor* is released internationally. Tian Zhuangzhuang's film *Rock 'n' Roll Youth* is released.

1989: 15 April, the death of Hu Yaobang sparks mass, nation-wide demonstrations against corruption, nepotism, as well as lobbying for press freedom and democracy. Students and workers demonstrate outside the New China Gate entrance of the Lake Palaces. On 4 June, the PLA crushes the protests and occupies Tiananmen Square under the force of arms. The ousted Party General Secretary, Zhao Ziyang, is 'cast into a cold palace' and dies in confinement in January 2005.

1996: the exhibition *Empress Dowager Cixi: Her Art of Living* is held in Hong Kong prior to the return of the former British colony to Chinese control the following year. Leung Ping-kwan writes his poem 'Cauldron'.

1998: September, Puccini's opera *Turandot* is performed at the Ancestral Temple.

1999: 25 April, the Lake Palaces are surrounded by protesters of the Falun Gong religious sect. The Millennium Monument is built in the west of Beijing to usher in the new century.

2001: June, the Three Tenors perform in front of the Meridian Gate.

2002: the National Qing History Committee commences work on an official history of China's last dynasty, to be published in 2014. A mock funeral is held at the Ancestral Temple as part of Feng Xiaogang's film *The Player*.

2003: the television series *Towards the Republic* portrays the Empress Dowager Cixi in a more positive light.

2004: the Eternally Fixed Gate, the original entrance to the Outer City of Beijing, is rebuilt as part of the north–south re-orientation of the city.

2006: May, the rebuilt Palace of Established Happiness in the north-west corner of the Forbidden City is opened.

2007: July, the Starbucks outlet in the former Office for the Nine Ministers is forced out of the Forbidden City. 8 August, celebrations in Tiananmen Square mark the year before the opening ceremony of the 29th Olympiad in Beijing. 11 December, *The Secret History of the Qing Court* (1948), denounced in 1950, screened in Beijing.

2008: the restored Hall of Supreme Harmony is opened to the public. Further restorations within the Forbidden City are planned to continue up to 2020, the 600th anniversary of the palace.

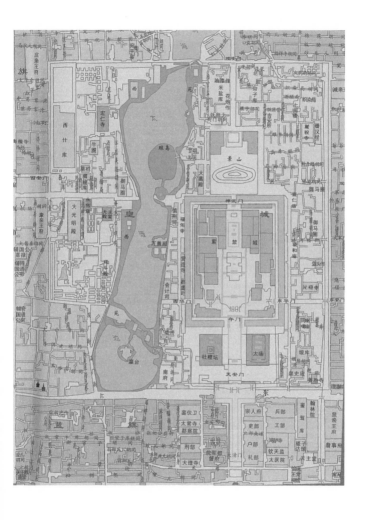

1. Plan of the Forbidden City showing the Forbidden City on the right and the Lake Palaces on the left.

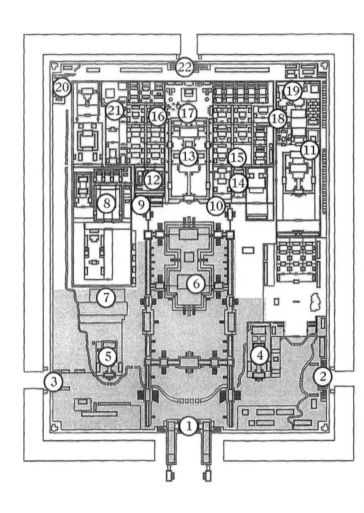

2. The Outer and Inner Court of the Forbidden City. The Outer Court is marked by grey shading.

KEY

3. Looking through China Gate along the Corridor of a Thousand Paces to the Gate of Heavenly Peace. China Gate was originally called Great Qing Gate after the last dynasty, and renamed following the 1911 Revolution. The gate was demolished during the expansion of Tiananmen Square in the 1950s and a mausoleum for Mao Zedong was built on the site in 1977.

I

....

A PALACE OF BLOOD AND TEARS

In the early hours of 18 August 1966, Chairman Mao Zedong and other leaders of the Chinese Communist Party emerged from the Gate of Heavenly Peace (*Tiananmen*), the inner gate of the Imperial City (*Huang Cheng*) that led to the Forbidden City. Nearly a million people had crowded into Tiananmen Square to attend the first mass rally of the Cultural Revolution.

Previously, under the emperors, major imperial edicts had been promulgated annually from the Gate of Heavenly Peace having been conveyed there in a golden casket by court officials from the main audience hall. But the last imperial edict had been issued in February 1912, in the name of the optimistically entitled Xuantong Emperor ('proclaimed continuity', r. 1909–11), a six-year-old boy called Aisin Gioro Puyi. It had announced his abdication and had transferred sovereignty to the people of China. With this edict the Great Qing dynasty that had ruled in Beijing for 268 years came to an end, as did a political system that had held sway over the country for over two millennia.

From the nineteenth century, the Forbidden City had come to embody the politics and culture, indeed the entire panoply of tradition, against which rebels and revolutionaries struggled for over a hundred years. In the twentieth century

it would haunt politicians and activists who found themselves enmeshed in the complex legacy of imperial power.
The responses to it of power-holders – be they democratic,
autocratic, revolutionary or reformist – as well as of thinkers of every persuasion tell a history of modern China itself.
The vacated throne of the main audience hall, the Hall of
Supreme Harmony (*Taihe Dian*), became a metaphor for a
past that had lost its authority – an image much favoured
by writers and academics. At the same time it occupied the
imagination of those who attempted to trace the skein of
connections between the dynastic history of China and its
modern transformations. Throughout their rule, Mao and
his supporters would use the symbols and language of the
dynastic past and convert them into elements of their own
political performances and vocabulary. They employed tradition when it suited them and repudiated it when the need
arose. The Forbidden City, empty since the expulsion in 1924
of the abdicated Xuantong Emperor, served as a backdrop,
both physical and symbolic, to the Maoist era from 1949 to
1976. The Forbidden City and the China that it represented,
however, retained a power that was not so easily dispelled.
While its buildings were subject to decay and change, the
China of secretive politics, rigid political codes and autocratic
behaviour continued to exert an influence far beyond the walls
of the former palace.

In 1912, the Qing dynasty was replaced by the Republic of
China, a fragile democracy that would soon fall prey to the
pressures of external invasion, internal corruption and a mass
insurgency led by the Communists. Nearly forty years after
the end of imperial rule, on 1 October 1949, Mao Zedong proclaimed the establishment of the government of the People's

Republic of China from the Gate of Heavenly Peace to a cheering crowd of tens of thousands in Tiananmen Square. The square then covered only 40,000 square metres. Over the subsequent decade and a half it would be expanded to accommodate the mass rallies organised by the rulers of the new socialist state until it covered more than 400,000 square metres – five times the size of Moscow's Red Square.

In 1966, during the night of 17 August, the square had gradually filled with the largest number of people it had ever seen. A million students from Beijing's high schools and universities as well as teachers, workers and state employees gathered, as instructed, in anticipation of some momentous event. As Rae Yang, a young high school student from a once-prominent Beijing family, recalled:

When we saw the light of dawn, we felt as if this was the dawn of a new era for mankind. We felt that we were about to embark on an unprecedented revolution. It would bring about a society that was truly egalitarian and democratic, one without private property or selfish thoughts. A brand new society.

In the pre-dawn gloom, they stirred themselves with popular patriotic songs, including a new paean in praise of Mao Zedong as the guiding light of world revolution: 'We Look to the Pole Star in the Sky Above'. When the assembled crowd learned that Mao himself had emerged from the Gate of Heavenly Peace to join them at ground level – an unprecedented act by a ruler of China – they became hysterical and chanted rhythmically the traditional salutation to the Chinese emperor, the Son of Heaven: '*Wansui, wansui, wanwansui*', 'Ten Thousand Years of Long Life!'

[3]

As Mao was ushered into the midst of the throng, the loudspeakers placed strategically about the square crackled with the strains of the unofficial anthem, 'The East is Red':

> The East is red,
> The sun has risen,
> Mao Zedong has appeared in China.
> He is devoted to the people's happiness.
> *Hu-er-hai-yo*,
> He is the people's Great Saviour.

After waving, shaking hands and chatting with members of the crowd, Mao was led back to the rostrum of the Gate of Heavenly Peace. There he officiated over the first mass rally of Red Guards and the beginning of what became known as the 'Great Proletarian Cultural Revolution', a revolution within a revolution, one aimed at cleaving China from its imperial past once and for all.

The song's adulatory image of Mao as the nation's 'Pole Star' relates directly to the symbolism of the Forbidden City, called in Chinese *Zijin Cheng* – the 'Forbidden Walled City of the Pole Star', that star being the unmoving heavenly body around which all else rotated. The emperor, or Son of Heaven, was the figure around which 'all under heaven' (*tianxia*) (that is, the entire Chinese world) revolved. Although the Forbidden City would be a public museum, Mao and his colleagues located both the seat of government and their residences not far away in the Central and South Lake Palaces (*Zhongnan Hai*). These palaces, which occupy a large area along the western flank of the Forbidden City (see chapter 7), were built on the remains of the palace of the Mongol Yuan

4. 'Chairman Mao Reviews the Great Army of the Proletarian Cultural Revolution from the Gate of Heavenly Peace on 18 August 1966'. Mao is wearing a People's Liberation Army uniform and a Red Guard armband. Under his right arm an archway in Zhongshan Park, formerly the Altar of State, can be seen.

dynasty (1279–1368). The old grounds and villas of the Lake Palaces were also favoured by the Kangxi ('lasting prosperity', r. 1661–1722) and Qianlong ('enduring glory', r. 1736–96) emperors of the Qing dynasty and they were often used by them (see chapters 3 and 4). When she resided in the Forbidden City the Empress Dowager would also spend time in the Lake Palaces, and she lived there for a time. Indeed, she also died there. These palaces later provided a residence for Yuan Shikai, the first president of the Republic of China. They would come to play a key role in the history of the Forbidden City after the founding of the People's Republic of China.

Post-dynastic rulers celebrated their coming to power from the podium of the Gate of Heavenly Peace – before Mao proclaimed the establishment of a new China in 1949, Yuan Shikai had marked his inauguration as president in 1913 in that same place. But under the emperors ascent to the throne was conducted ceremonially within the Hall of Supreme Harmony. Unusually, in 1644, when the peasant rebel Li Zicheng (see chapter 7) sacked Beijing and occupied the palace, he ascended the throne in the Hall of Martial Valour (*Wuying Dian*) to the west of the Hall of Supreme Harmony. However, he was forced to flee the palace the very next day.

Resonances sound throughout the dynastic and post-dynastic histories of the Forbidden City. After the fall of the Qing dynasty, the Hall of Martial Valour, for example, housed the newly established Gallery of Antiquities (*Guwu Chenlie Suo*), the first museum in the palace (see chapter 6). In the early years of the People's Republic, the same building also played a significant role as a public space. In March 1950, the preparatory committee for the Central Museum of the

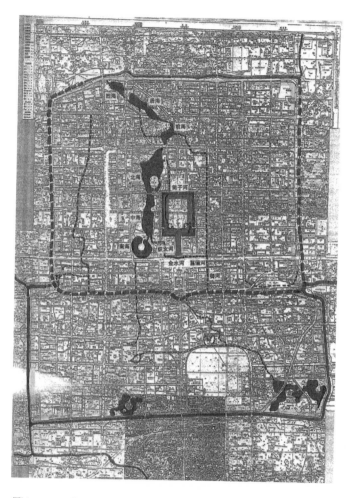

5. This map outlines the Outer City in the south, the Inner City to the north and within it the Imperial City, the walls of which were largely dismantled in the 1910s. This encloses the Forbidden City. The area of the Lake Palaces inside the Imperial City is clearly delineated.

Revolution took it over and, by the middle of that month, staged its first exhibition there. Reflecting the priorities and the prolixity of the revolutionary regime, the exhibition was entitled 'Crimes at the Concentration Camps of the American Imperialists and Chiang Kai-shek Bandits in Chongqing'. Other exhibitions in the Forbidden City followed: a display of revolutionary materials from the Qing dynasty in the Hall of Tender Mercy (*Benren Dian*); an exhibition of historical material related to imperialist aggression against China in the halls on top of the Meridian Gate (*Wu Men*); and a display of photographs and reports promoting China's military support for North Korea in what was called the 'Anti-US/Support Korea Campaign' mounted in the Hall of Supreme Harmony. Only after the radical enthusiasm of the first years of the People's Republic had waned was the Forbidden City gradually reclaimed as a cultural institution for the display of antiquities.

The new Communist government, however, was determined to repudiate or transform China's decadent and feudal past. It effectively declared war on old Beijing, deeming its lifestyle of leisure, culture and consumption to be the hallmarks of Manchu decadence, supine betrayal of the national interest and the source of China's humiliation. All this had its epicentre in the Forbidden City. Even during the early days of the previous Republic of China, debate had raged over where to locate the capital of a new, avowedly democratic China. In the 1910s, the constitutional monarchist-*cum*-reformer Liang Qichao remarked:

> *The capital Beijing has become the hotbed of all evils. Not only has the land lost its pleasing features and the water its sweet taste*

but a thousand crimes, a myriad of scandals, and all the weird carbuncles and chronic diseases of this sinful world are concentrated there. If the political centre stays in Beijing, China will never see a single day of clean government.

The Communists were well aware of the Imperial City's complex and, for them and other twentieth-century revolutionaries, odious legacy. They declared it their aim to transform the capital. No longer would it be a city that fed off the nation's resources; they would turn it into a centre of production. However, when they drew up the plans for new Beijing, the ineluctable fact that the Forbidden City took up more than 72 hectares at the very centre of the capital of a new, socialist China could not be avoided. The palace was a tangible symbol of the reactionary and feudal past; its presence was a palpable obstacle to revolutionary modernization. Stubbornly occupying the heart of the city, it also blocked the flow of traffic and people.

In 1949, the architects Liang Sicheng and Chen Zhanxiang presented the Communist Party leaders with a city plan. Liang, who was the son of Liang Qichao, quoted above, was one of the founders of China's first architectural association, as well as being on the panel which designed the headquarters of the United Nations in New York. He had long studied the magnificent layout of Beijing and declared that it was 'a peerless masterpiece of urban planning'. In what was dubbed the ''49 Scheme', Liang and Chen proposed a new municipal centre located outside the western walls of the old city where the Japanese had had their military headquarters during their occupation of the former capital in the 1930s and 1940s. The seat of their civil administration was the old municipal government offices at the Lake Palaces. Under Liang and Chen's plan the old city would be preserved with a public park laid out along its walls, and the modern city still taking the Forbidden City as its centre.

In 1952, the central government rejected the "49 Scheme', and a vociferous debate ensued over designs for the new city and the role in it of the Forbidden City. For the moment the seat of government was in the Lake Palaces, and the basic principle underlying the mooted plans was that the headquarters of the Party bureaucracy and the national government should remain in the centre of the capital. At a planning meeting in July 1953, the mayor of Beijing, Peng Zhen, unilaterally declared that the majority of the population favoured demolishing the old city walls, preserving only the Forbidden City and its major antique structures. The meeting proposed that the headquarters of the Communist Party and the People's Government be located in grand new edifices in the Soviet style to be built on or near the original imperial-era ministries around an expanded Tiananmen Square. As the hub of the city shifted south, the heroic multi-storeyed structures of the new socialist China would overshadow the Forbidden City itself.

While debates and discussions on this proposal continued behind closed doors, Party apparatchiki organized 'the masses' of Beijing to agitate in favour of Peng Zhen's proposal. The resulting 'vox populi' reports were published in the press, supposedly discrediting as 'élitist', 'out-of-touch' and 'unrepresentative' the views of architectural historians, academics, cultural activists and the original inhabitants who loved the old city. Moreover, despite obligatory discussions with experts and nominal consideration of the city's cultural heritage, Peng Zhen had by then learned that the Chairman disliked old Beijing and that he wanted to see it torn down and rebuilt. All that held back implementation of the more drastic proposals of the 1950s was a lack of money.

In January 1958, at a meeting of the Party's Central Committee in Nanning, Guangxi province, Mao unabashedly expressed his views:

They did a good job of demolishing the city walls of [the old provincial capitals] Nanjing, Jinan and Changsha. It would be best if all the old buildings of Beijing and Kaifeng [in Henan province] were replaced with new ones ... But I should add, there are people who criticise me for being obsessed with grandiose plans. They claim I'm biased in my views and only favour certain opinions. They say that I suffer violent mood swings and that I have no regard for antiquities. Well, they're right. I do like the grandiose. As for antiquities, you can enjoy them, but not too much. It is quite right for people not to love relics. If I did, then we'd be having today's meeting at Zhoukoudian [the cave system near Beijing where the remains of Peking Man were discovered].

Others were sceptical that the destruction of bricks and mortar would result in the fundamental reinvention of the nation or a meaningful disavowal of its feudal legacy. To them the Forbidden City and its celestial geometry symbolised and oriented old Beijing itself.

The debate over the fate of the Forbidden City was to continue for years. The most dramatic proposals to alter, transform or even level the palace came on the eve of the tenth anniversary of the People's Republic. In April 1958, Premier

Zhou Enlai reported Mao Zedong's instructions that over the coming years Beijing was to undergo a complete transformation. Although the fraternal socialist state relationship between China and the Soviet Union would soon sour, the Soviet reconstruction of Moscow weighed heavily in the calculations of the Chinese leaders. They too craved a vast space like Red Square for their self-congratulatory parades; and they wanted to live and work within their own equivalent of the Kremlin. 'The Forbidden City was built for the old emperors,' Peng Zhen now declared. 'Why can't we transform it into the offices of the Central Government?' Zhao Pengfei, one of those who had lobbied for the creation of Tiananmen Square, even suggested building the State Council's offices on the square itself. However, enthusiasm for a radical break with the material legacy of the past was not confined to the revolutionary leaders. By this time the city's population had swelled dramatically with Party followers and internal migrants from other provinces. Many held the old walled city in contempt and participated in the new wave of destruction with revolutionary fervour. Tens of thousands of Beijing citizens, new and old, were mobilised to demolish the city gates and walls in a process of scarification that was to continue into the late 1960s. Volunteers participated in the construction of the Ten Great Edifices (*Shi Dajianzhu*) that were built at Tiananmen Square, along Chang'an Boulevard and elsewhere in the city to mark the tenth anniversary of the People's Republic. Many nursed a passionate hope that a bright socialist future would rise from the ruins of the past.

While the early socialist urban planners expended their energies on reorienting the geometric imperial layout of the city (thereby creating aesthetic and other problems only

6. A Plan for Tiananmen Square from 1954. This was one of the many proposals considered by the Party authorities redesigning the centre of Beijing. In the foreground is the Front Gate of the Inner City and the Noonday Gate. In the middle is a new Chinese Communist Party Central Office designed in the Soviet style and flanked by government ministries. The new buildings would have eclipsed the Gate of Heavenly Peace and the Forbidden City beyond.

tentatively addressed in revised urban plans of the early twenty-first century, some fifty years too late), and despite the frequent formulation of new plans, the Forbidden City remained relatively tranquil and untouched. But there was continued disquiet. After the completion of the Museum of the History of the Revolution and the Great Hall of the People on the east and west sides of the expanded Tiananmen Square as part of the celebrations of the first decade of the People's Republic, classified Communist Party documents cited anonymous workers in Beijing who derided the Forbidden City as 'too empty and quite ugly'. 'It's useless,' they claimed, 'and not in sympathy with all the new buildings on Tiananmen Square.'

A new ten-year plan for the reconstruction of central Beijing announced in February 1960 declared that an east–west highway should be built in front of the Meridian Gate, the main entrance to the Forbidden City. It called for the side buildings of the Hall of Martial Valour and the Hall of Literary Flourishing (*Wenhua Dian*) to be converted into activity centres for the 'masses'. By that time, however, the effects of the Great Leap Forward were rippling throughout China. Calamitous economic dislocation resulting from utopian policies aimed at realising industrial and agrarian communism overnight contributed to the largest manmade famine in history. People did not have enough to eat, let alone the time or energy to destroy any more imperial palaces. It was a time when, as the saying went, 'flower pots were broken and vegetables planted' (*za huapen'r, zhong shucai*). In an act that reflected his appreciation of the disaster the Party's policies had visited on the country, Mao even ordered the digging up of the ornamental plants and ancient trees at his own residence, the Garden of Abundant Nourishment (*Fengze Yuan*) in the Lake Palaces; by the early 1960s the imperial courtyard gardens where Kangxi had grown mulberry trees and carried out experiments in rice cultivation were producing corn, sorghum, tomatoes and chillies. Mao enjoined other central leaders to follow his example and give up the cultivation of flowers and non-productive vegetation in their compounds in favour of vegetables, even if the act was symbolic at best. Even the gardens of the Fishing Terrace State Guesthouse (*Diaoyu Tai Guobin Guan*), an imperial detached palace to the west of the city, were dug up and replanted.

By 1964, the economy had recovered sufficiently for the destruction to resume: a dramatically widened highway – Chang'an Boulevard (*Chang'an Jie*) – running through the centre of Beijing in front of the Gate of Heavenly Peace would bifurcate the north–south axis of the city. Another east–west road was planned to cut through the Forbidden City itself. Within a year, however, the unprecedented political and social turmoil of the Cultural Revolution was sweeping the country and plans to bulldoze the approaches to the palace had to be abandoned.

The Forbidden City was thus the accidental beneficiary of the two most harrowing episodes of recent Chinese history: the Great Leap Forward during which tens of millions died of starvation, and the Great Proletarian Cultural Revolution which otherwise saw the wholesale devastation of the country's tangible cultural heritage through Party-sponsored iconoclasm and callous mismanagement. These events put paid to plans to build a Chairman's Office facing the palace, and to construct an expressway in front of the Meridian Gate.

But the Forbidden City did not escape entirely unscathed.

In May 1966, as the Cultural Revolution was unfolding, the Central Logistics Department of the People's Liberation Army (PLA) dispatched a work team to the former palace. Their programme for renovation included erecting two mammoth columns bearing quotations from Chairman Mao in the forecourt of the former imperial throne room, the Hall of Supreme Harmony. Taller than the hall itself, the totemic structures would, in the words of their army designers, 'disrupt the imperial pretence of feudalism'. Furthermore, they would remove the imperial throne and arrange a sculptural tableau in front of the empty dais depicting a heroic group of rebellious peasants menacing a terrified emperor with their halberds.

They also planned to remove the throne in the next chamber, the Hall of Central Harmony (*Zhonghe Dian*), which had been a resting place for the emperor during audiences, and convert the place into the People's Lounge (*Renmin Xiuxishi*). And, in an attempt to carry out a 'rectification of names', they would replace all of the plaques hanging over the entryways to the halls and palaces of the Forbidden City whose names had feudal connotations with portraits of Mao Zedong.

By July 1966, the People's Lounge was open. Where the imperial throne had once stood were now ten chairs around a long table on which several newspapers were placed. In this institutional reading room, revolutionary museum workers could attempt to fathom the latest directives emanating from across the walls in the Lake Palaces. Just as the plaques were being removed, Red Guards attempted to invade the palace intent on 'destroying the Four Olds of the exploiting classes': old ideas, culture, customs and habits. The Party's programme for the Cultural Revolution called for

7. 'A Palace of Blood and Tears'. The couplet on either side of the Gate of Divine Prowess reads: 'Stamp out the old world of emperors, generals and ministers' (right) and 'Create a new world in which seven hundred million people are [like the sage kings] Shun and Yao' (left). Underneath the new name of the palace are the words 'To Rebel is Justified'.

the obliteration of the remnants of the 'feudal and bour-geois' past. A line from one of Mao's poems was quoted *ad nauseam*: 'The Golden Monkey wrathfully swung his massive cudgel,/And the jade-like firmament was cleared of dust'. For the people of Beijing, the eighth month of 1966 was to become known as 'bloody August', during which time – and in the months that followed – Red Guards wreaked havoc as they went about destroying the Four Olds throughout the capital – temples, statues, churches, religious texts, street signs, shop fronts, private collections of books, antiques, even family photographs and papers. They also wanted to vent their ire on the most tangible remnant of China's feudal past, the Forbidden City.

Although palace staff managed to turn back the rebels, another group at the northern entrance succeeded in erect-ing a sign over the main gate that read 'A Palace of Blood and Tears' (*Xuelei Gong*). Red Guards joined by rebellious and disaffected palace employees painted the couplet 'Stamp out the old world of emperors, generals and ministers' and 'Create a new world in which seven hundred million people are [equal to the ancient sage kings] Shun and Yao' on either side of the gateway in the outer wall.

Even on the eve of the mass rally of 18 August, groups of Red Guards milled in the courtyard outside the Meridian Gate demanding entry to the palace. They wanted to destroy what they saw as the symbol of the forces that had made traditional China poor and weak. Party leaders, including Premier Zhou Enlai, however, were unwilling to acquiesce in the complete destruction of the city's cultural heritage. They ordered museum workers in the Forbidden City complex to refuse the Red Guards entry. At the same time, however, elderly curators inside the palace were being subjected to the same psychological and physical tortures as other 'reactionary bourgeois authorities' throughout the country.

The Palace Museum thereafter remained closed for much of the Cultural Revolution, even as a museum exhibit was made of its deputy director, Shan Shiyuan. Revolutionary rebels among his younger colleagues attacked him as a 'reactionary authority' and he was put on public display in the Hall for Worshipping Ancestors (*Fengxian Dian*) (now the Imperial Clock Exhibit). As part of the movement to increase awareness of the ever-present dangers of class struggle, sculptors in Sichuan had created *The Rent Collection Courtyard* in 1965, a massive 100-metre-long work on the subject of the exploitation of the labouring masses in the old society, and the ancient hall had to be redesigned to accommodate it. Divided into dramatic chapters with over 100 individual sculptures it was hailed by the Chinese art world as a 'cultural atom bomb'. Shan, who bore an uncanny resemblance to Liu Wencai, the evil landlord who was the central villain in the sculptural work, was told to stand next to it with a placard hung around his neck that read 'A Living Liu Wencai, the faithful descendant of the feudal emperors, and reactionary academic authority'. Visitors, who numbered in the thousands, were encouraged to abuse him verbally and force him to chant slogans. Despite explicit instructions to the contrary, many felt they also had licence to spit on him or even administer a few slaps. Out-of-town Red Guards who streamed into the capital during the early months of the Cultural Revolution were even more brutal than the local breed of rebellious lout. One group beat the old curator so badly that he partially lost the vision in one eye. Only then did the authorities put a stop to the vicious

8. The Hall of the Ancestors. This building was redesigned and connected to the pavilion behind it so as to accommodate the revolutionary sculptural work, *The Rent Collection Courtyard*. It was here that Shan Shiyuan, a veteran curator and deputy director of the Palace Museum, was subjected to Red Guard taunts and violence. The building now houses the Imperial Clock Exhibit.

scapegoating. According to his daughter, Shan neither forgot nor forgave the cruel indignity.

The destructive frenzy aimed at the palace was not limited to impotent sloganeering and the manhandling of curatorial staff. On 2 August 1966, workers at the Cultural Relics Publishing House smashed all of the clay statues in the eighteenth-century Temple of the City God (*Chenghuang Miao*) by the moat in the north-west corner of the palace. The publishing house had located its printing press in the temple some years earlier and, in an official report to the PLA team in charge of the palace, the workers explained that they were responding to Chairman Mao's call to rebel against the reactionary *status quo*. They claimed that the old statues were 'spirit kings and little devils that must be thoroughly smashed along with the anti-Party anti-socialist blackguards. We cannot allow such evil creatures to occupy such a respected place. We must uproot all feudal things that have been used to harm the people for thousands of years.' The authorities sanctioned their iconoclasm, saying that the images in the temple were of crude craftsmanship, of recent provenance (dating merely from the mid-Qing dynasty) and of no cultural merit. (To this day the temple remains closed to the public. The printery eventually fell under the jurisdiction of the Palace Museum and until recently the buildings housed the offices of its official magazine, *Zijin Cheng*.)

These events and the spread of factional violence led the State Council to close the Palace Museum from 16 August 1966, just two days before that first Red Guard mass rally in Tiananmen Square. However, threats to the palace continued unabated. Red Guards from the nearby city of Tianjin even attempted to ram the doors at the north entrance of the

[21]

Forbidden City with a truck. Finally, Premier Zhou Enlai felt obliged to dispatch a battalion of troops to live in the palace. This occupying force would visit its own careless depredations on it.

Meanwhile, in a twist as confounding as any imperial intrigue, the PLA work team that had been busy tearing out thrones in its own ruinous transfiguration of the palace now found itself denounced. It had not been radical enough, apparently, and now it was being attacked for supposedly having pursued a 'bourgeois reactionary line'. With the Palace Museum closed to the public, and the staff inflamed with revolutionary zeal and busy with rallies and political meetings, the People's Lounge fell into abeyance and the slogan towers and plans for new sculptures in the Hall of Supreme Harmony were postponed indefinitely. Over the following years, changing political priorities saw a revolutionary committee take charge of the palace led by people with little appreciation for either the Forbidden City's past or its value. They subjected curators and workers to the relentless study of Mao Zedong Thought, endless rounds of political rallies and periods of 're-education through manual labour' in the countryside.

For many employees of the Palace Museum the Cultural Revolution came to an unofficial end late one night in September 1970 when Premier Zhou Enlai paid a surprise visit and instructed them to get ready to re-open within a year. He did not tell them why, but he had issued the order in anticipation of an official visit to China by the President of the United States Richard Nixon. The Palace Museum opened for a US ping-pong team in Beijing at Zhou's invitation in April 1971. It would formally open its doors on 5 July that year, although the revolutionary committee remained in charge until January 1973.

The Nixon trip to China was momentous in many ways. While Nixon was bored by his tour of the Forbidden City – totally unaware of the anxious preparations that had gone into its re-opening since the forced closure five years earlier – its symbolism played a role in the US–China rapprochement. Nixon's Secretary of State and secret emissary to China, Henry Kissinger, even used the palace metaphorically to describe the historic encounter between the long-disaffected countries. During Nixon's trip to Beijing, he had a summit with Mao, during which the Chairman was at his gnomic best, leaving the American side a little baffled and disappointed. Kissinger wrote:

Later on, as I comprehended better the many-layered design of Mao's conversation, I understood that it was like the courtyards in the Forbidden City, each leading to a deeper recess distinguished from the others only by slight changes of proportion, with ultimate meaning residing in a totality that only long reflection could grasp.

Such metaphors continued to mark Western interpretations of China, and of interactions with China's leaders. The image of the 'secretive enigma' of the country lived on. Meanwhile, the refurbishment of the Forbidden City for the Nixon visit marked the beginning of the history of the palace as an accessible international tourist attraction.

Even though no longer the seat of power, the Forbidden City remained at the physical and emblematic centre of Chinese politics throughout the twentieth century. But it had been built to be far more than just a symbol of power or a drawcard for tourists; in its very design it was conceived to awe, inspire and instruct.

THE ARCHITECTURE OF
HIERARCHY

The Yongle Emperor ('perpetual happiness', r. 1403–24) had imperial designs long before he became emperor. A son of the founder of the Ming dynasty, he had been made the Prince of Yan, Yan being the ancient name for Beijing and the surrounding region. There he took up residence in the extensive palaces of the 'Mighty Khan' of the Mongol Yuan dynasty (1279–1368) and plotted to unseat his nephew, the Jianwen Emperor ('establishing the civil', r. 1399–1402) whom he regarded as ineffectual.

When the Ming rulers had conquered the old Mongol capital of Dadu ('the great capital') in 1368 they had renamed it Beiping ('the north pacified'). The Mongol palaces there were called the 'Great Within' (*Da Nei*) and the famed Venetian traveller Marco Polo described the central audience hall of them as 'the greatest Palace that ever was'. His account reads as though it were written for a travel brochure for today's Forbidden City:

> *The building is altogether so vast, so rich and so beautiful, that no man on earth could design anything superior to it. The outside of the roof is all coloured with vermilion and yellow and blue and*

[25]

other hues, which are fixed with a varnish so fine and exquisite that they shine like crystal, and lend a resplendent lustre to the palace as seen for a great way round. This roof is made too with such strength and solidity that it is fit to last for ever.

After he usurped the throne, the new Yongle Emperor moved the capital of the Ming dynasty from Nanjing ('the southern capital') to his powerbase in the former Mongol Yuan dynastic city in the north. When he commanded the move he also changed the name of the city from Beiping to Beijing ('the northern capital') and ordered the construction of an extensive new palace, the Forbidden City. The building of the palace lasted from 1416 to 1420. The name 'Forbidden City' (*Zijin Cheng*), however, only appeared in 1576, more than 150 years after Yongle's death. Yongle remained ensconced in the Mongol palaces until his own new and much-expanded 'Great Within' was completed, whereupon he ordered the old palaces to be demolished. Part of the site would become an imperial garden called the Lake Palaces (see chapter 7).

Writers confine the inspiration for the Forbidden City and its grand architecture solely to the culture and peoples of China Proper (*Zhong Yuan*, literally the 'Central Plains'). As a result, people are generally unaware of the important Mongol contribution to its design. This is ironic considering that no Chinese imperial palace constructed before or since the Great Within, created by the 'barbarian' Yuan dynasty, has conformed so closely to the precepts governing imperial architecture as set out in the canonical text *The Rites of Zhou* (*Zhou Li*). This book, dating from the second century BCE, prescribes protocols and regulations governing the scale and attributes of architecture, housing, clothing, jewellery, vehicles, sacrifices, funerary accessories and accoutrements for the emperor and all social estates. Its later permutations included meticulous codes and rules that governed in minute detail the behaviour of the denizens of the palace, in particular eunuchs and palace women and so created an inviolable human architecture of hierarchy. The Mongols followed it rigorously in their design of their Great Within and the Yongle Emperor drew his inspiration from that palace.

The entrance of the Forbidden City is straddled by the Meridian Gate, its builders intending it to overawe all those who passed through it. Towering above the north–south axis along which the palace complex is symmetrically arranged and which runs through the centre of the dragon throne, the Meridian Gate was named after the central longitude of the ancient Chinese compass. Signifying true south, true north and high noon, it had the power to impress and even intimidate emissaries of tributary states with the might of empire.

From the gate's parapets, emperors presided over military ceremonies and victory parades, as well as the annual proclamation of the calendar which determined agricultural and ritual activities throughout the empire. One of the greatest victories of the Qing dynasty during its rise as a continental empire was the defeat by the Qianlong Emperor's armies in 1755 of the Muslim Mongols in Turkestan. This victory was consolidated four years later when the heads of the last two rebellious sultans, known as the Elder Khodja and Younger Khodja, were presented to the Manchu general Fude. The heads were conveyed to Qianlong in Beijing, where, on 12 March 1760, from the Meridian Gate, he reviewed the troops displaying their prisoners of war in the courtyard below. Taking grisly comfort in the trophy beside him – a casket containing the left ears of the two Khodjas – he wrote a poem celebrating the occasion:

The casketed Khodjas heads are brought from desert caves;
The devoted Sultan knocks at palace gates …
By Western Lakes, the might of Qing Eternal is decided,
At the Meridian Gate our triumph is thrice proclaimed.
From this day forth, we no longer stay this military course,
My people, sharing joyful plenitude, now shall take their rest.

Rising to a height of over 35 metres, the Meridian Gate was the tallest structure in the Forbidden City and the Imperial City that surrounded it. No building was permitted to exceed it in height. Indeed, the Meridian Gate and the southern gates of the Imperial City, in particular the Gate of Heavenly Peace, dominated the cityscape of the capital well into the twentieth century. In *Peking Picnic*, a 1932 romantic novel set against a backdrop of diplomatic life in Beijing in the late 1920s, its author, Ann Bridge, describes how 'the great red gateways stood up in the evening light like immense double-decker Noah's Arks roofed in golden tiles'.

The Meridian Gate echoed in grand style the ancient gates with watchtowers (*que*) which the Han dynasty had built twelve centuries earlier. Necropolis architecture incorporated such gates as the symbolic entrance to heaven for the souls of the aristocrats entombed within. In their subterranean carved or painted versions, these gates were often coupled with imagery of the twin emblems of imperial power – the dragon and the phoenix. This earned for the Meridian Gate the nickname the 'Five Phoenix Towers' (*Wufeng Lou*)

9. The Qianlong Emperor reviewing a victory parade from the Meridian Gate (see also the cover image). After ceremonies at the Ancestral Temple and the Altar of State, prisoners of war would be displayed to the emperor here whereupon he would decide their fate. During the Ming dynasty, floggings (*ting zhang*) of officials who had raised imperial ire were carried out on the east side of the courtyard of this gate.

because five pavilions were built on its uppermost level. (The largest of these is now an exhibition hall.)

Although its designers conceived of the Meridian Gate, completed in 1420, as sealing an impregnable enclosure, it fulfilled no real military function. The palace was invaded a number of times. The Wala Mongols occupied the complex in 1447 for a short time; Li Zicheng's rebel armies and the Manchus followed in 1644 (see chapter 7), as did the Heavenly Principle religious sect rebels in 1813; an Anglo-French force imposed themselves on it for a time in 1860, and the Eight-Power Allied Expedition was to encounter little opposition on entering and plundering the royal keep in 1900 (see chapter 5). While today's patriotic historians tend to characterise the Forbidden City of the Ming and Qing dynasties as having enjoyed an uninterrupted continuum of imperial occupancy, in fact throughout its history many of the palace buildings within the Forbidden City have lain either vacant or in ruins.

The Meridian Gate played a role in the rituals of the new palace. Three passageways with red-lacquered doors and metal studs pierce the gate. The central archway was reserved for the use of the emperor, who came and went borne in a yellow palanquin. The three top graduates in the most recent imperial examinations were given the honour of being allowed to leave the palace through this central arch, while foreign ambassadors granted an audience within the Forbidden City itself, at least during the Ming and the earliest years of the Qing, also entered via the central gate.

Once through the gate, the visitor enters a large forecourt through which a canal called the River of Golden Waters (*Jinshui He*) runs sinuously along a gleaming marble bed. The *fengshui*, or geomantic arrangement of auspicious sites,

10. The Gate of Supreme Harmony and the Hall of Supreme Harmony during reconstruction, seen from the Meridian Gate. Prospect Hill is visible to the north.

requires water to flow in front and a mountain to rise protectively at the rear. The 'mountain' of the Forbidden City is Prospect Hill (*Jing Shan*), an artificial mound built up by Yongle using the soil and rocks removed following the excavation of the Forbidden City's moat.

Passing through a second parallel gate on the north–south axis, the Gate of Supreme Harmony (*Taihe Men*), the visitor proceeds to a broad court in which ministers gathered according to their ranks, as indicated by markers on the flagstones. The court is dominated by the towering Hall of Supreme Harmony, a building that appears to float in the light. Its stepped marble platforms and ornate balustrades are named 'Mount Sumeru stages' (*Xumi zuo*) after the mountain which stands at the centre of the universe in Buddhist cosmology. On the third and highest level are a bronze crane and turtle which signify perpetuity, or longevity, and near them two huge gilded bronze vats which denote purity.

Constructing the Hall of Supreme Harmony was a monumental undertaking. Woodsmen braving the tiger-ridden forests of Sichuan province harvested gigantic trunks of the close-grained and fragrant hardwood *Phoebe nanmu* and floated them down the Yangtze river for the columns of the hall, while other timbers were brought from the mountain forests of Guizhou and Hubei provinces along the Grand Canal. Kilns established at *Liuli Chang*, literally the Glazed-tile Factory (now Beijing's foremost street of antiquarian book stores and antique and curio shops), produced the vast numbers of tiles needed to roof and decorate all the palaces of the Forbidden City. The buildings were paved with dark 'metal bricks' from the south, so called because they reverberated when struck.

By 1420, what is today known as the Hall of Supreme Harmony and the other major buildings of the Yongle Emperor's Great Within were complete, the work supervised by the Annamese eunuch Nguyen An and the Minister of Public Works, Wu Zhong. Then, in 1421, less than 100 days after the Hall of Supreme Harmony was inaugurated, violent electrical storms struck Beijing and lightning severely damaged the ceremonial halls. Vocal scholar bureaucrats who had opposed the move north memorialised the throne and decried the wealth lavished on the new imperial city. Claiming that the lightning strikes were the heaven-sent punishment of imperial hubris, they called on the emperor to reflect on his errors and extravagance. One of their number, a scholar by the name of Li Shimian, even wrote, 'I for one would gladly accompany you when and if you decide to return to Nanjing and to report to your father at his tomb about the natural calamities.' The Yongle Emperor was unmoved by the chorus of protests and Li was cast into jail. Work on lavish imperial projects continued so that, by the end of the Ming dynasty, the rare timbers favoured by the imperial court – *zitan* ('red sandalwood') and *nanmu* – were virtually extinct. When the Kangxi Emperor came to rebuild the Hall of Supreme Harmony in 1695, he had to be content with columns of pine. (Although the original plans have been lost, Kangxi's own meticulous designs have survived and served as the guide for the total reconstruction of the hall from 2006 to 2008.)

The Hall of Supreme Harmony was the most important hall in the palace, the venue for coronations, or more precisely 'enthronements' (*deng ji*), and major imperial birthday celebrations. Prior to 1789, the final round of the government recruitment examinations, called the 'palace examinations' (*dian shi*), also took place here. Behind the main hall stands the smaller Hall of Central Harmony, most recently rebuilt in 1765. It has a square shape, with windows on all sides. At its centre is a throne, flanked by sedan chairs, and this is where the emperor would rest and refresh himself before presiding over major events in the Hall of Supreme Harmony. The third building on this axis is the Hall of Preserving Harmony (*Baohe Dian*), a banquet hall for the heads of tribute missions from the Ming through to the early Qing period.

The imperial aesthetic of cosmic perfection is exemplified by these three halls in the Forbidden City's Outer Court (*Wai Chao*). It was there that the court conducted most of its formal rituals but, over time, increasingly less of the business of government. The Hall of Supreme Harmony offers the dominant note in the symphony of vermilion walls, golden tiles and grey courtyards which unify the exterior architecture of the Forbidden City (although during the Ming many of the buildings not on the central axis were tiled in green). Only the roof of one of the imperial libraries in the palace, the Pavilion of Literary Profundity (*Wenyuan Ge*), was covered with black glazed tiles, a colour related to the element of water within the ancient Chinese ordering of the universe, which would help vouchsafe the books of the collection. This ordering of the world saw a correlation between the Five Elements (wood, fire, earth, metal and water), the Five Directions (east, south, centre, west and north), the Five Colours (green/blue, red, yellow, white and black) and the Five Musical Notes. Together with integers and zodiac signs, these categories inform the architectural codes of classical Chinese architecture, which also encompass elements drawn from numerology, divination and geomancy. Every measurement and design feature of the buildings and court-yards in the Forbidden City reflects a holistic approach to its architecture aimed at harmonising the forces of heaven, man and earth for the sake of dynastic stability and the prosperity of the realm.

Each dynasty took one of the elements and a corresponding colour to best exemplify its attributes. While the imperial colour of the Ming dynasty which rose in the south was red and its ruling element wood, the Qing dynasty from the north had black for its imperial colour and its element was water. According to the traditional interplay of *yin-yang* and the Five Elements, the natural 'enemy' of wood was water. Numbers were also significant, and auspicious meanings were attached to their pronunciation. 'Nine' (*jiu* 九) was a homonym for 'longevity' (*jiu* 久); nine was also the highest integer. The roofs of buildings for the exclusive use of the emperor feature nine auspicious creatures, finial figures that descend in order down their ridges to the corner. The builders of the Hall of Supreme Harmony added one extra figurine to the procession, rendering that building unique. It was also the broadest structure in the Forbidden City and the empire. The original Ming building was nine 'bays' (*jian*) wide – a bay being the roof span between two supporting columns. The Kangxi-era reconstruction extended it to eleven bays in order to accommodate fire prevention walls. This was balanced against a depth of five 'bays', the maximum to which traditional modular Chinese architecture could extend given the weight of the tiled roofs and ornate eaves of buildings, including the two-tonne 'dragon kisses' (*long wen*) that resemble dragons biting into the roof peak.

At the rear of the Hall of Preserving Harmony is a massive

inclined slab of stone set along the north–south axis of the palace and carved with precisely delineated dragons. This 'cinnabar stairway stone' (*danbi shi*), over which only the emperor could be carried in a palanquin, is the largest in the Forbidden City. Carved from a single immense piece of marble, it took more than 10,000 labourers and 6,000 troops to transport it from the imperial quarries in today's Fangshan district to Beijing's centre some fifty kilometres away along a specially constructed road. Wells were dug along the road at intervals of approximately half a kilometre and, in the dead heart of winter, the ice from those wells was used to slide the stone along a manmade glacis.

After presiding over major events of state, the emperor would descend from the Hall of Preserving Harmony over the cinnabar stairway stone to return to his living quarters in the Inner Court (*Nei Ting*) or Rear Palaces (*Hou Gong*), having passed through the Gate of Heavenly Purity (*Qianqing Men*) which divides the Forbidden City in half. Huge bronze vats are positioned at intervals on either side of the gate for storing water in case of fire, a constant threat to the flammable wooden buildings of the palace. The courtyard south of the Gate of Heavenly Purity is flanked on the east by the Gate of Good Fortune (*Jingyun Men*) and on the west by the Gate of the Prosperous Imperial House (*Longzhong Men*). The former leads to the Archery Pavilion (*Jian Ting*), built for martial contests, and on to the extensive eastern apartments built by the Qianlong Emperor for his retirement. The Gate of the Prosperous Imperial House opens on to palatial courtyards with luxurious apartments, temples and gardens which were once the preserve of imperial dowagers and retired consorts – the Palace of Benevolent Tranquillity

(*Cining Gong*), the Palace of Peaceful Longevity (*Shou'an Gong*) and the Palace of Longevity and Health (*Shoukang Gong*). (These now house the offices and storerooms of the Palace Museum and are closed to the public.)

At the eastern side of the Gate of Heavenly Purity was a small building called the Office for the Nine Ministers (*Jiuqing Fang*) (the site of a museum shop and, until July 2007, a Starbucks outlet). In the Qing dynasty, the emperor's leading officials assembled here before dawn after entering the Forbidden City through the East Flourishing Gate (*Donghua Men*) and prior to audiences and working sessions with the emperor.

The Outer Court was thus designed for the public activities of the emperor, and the Inner Court for the private lives of the imperial family. Traditionally, however, the arrangement of the Forbidden City is described as consisting of three parallel north–south bands or precincts called *lu*, meaning 'roads'. The Central Precinct (*Zhong Lu*) contains the Three Halls and the Three Rear Palaces (see below). The Western Precinct (*Xi Lu*) includes the Hall of Martial Valour, mentioned in chapter 1, which is located in the south-west corner; further north is the Imperial Household Department (*Neiwu Fu*) and the extensive palaces of dowagers and retired consorts mentioned above, with the Garden of the Palace of Established Happiness (*Jianfu Gong Huayuan*) in the north-west section. Also in this precinct are the apartments of the reigning emperor and those of his royal women. The Hall of Literary Flourishing in the southern part of the Eastern Precinct (*Dong Lu*) was where the heir-apparent received instruction in the classics and histories, and emperors dictated their treatises or disquisitions (*lun*) on philosophical and ethical matters to kneeling scribes. Further north in the Eastern Precinct was the 'mini Forbidden City' of Qianlong (see chapter 5), the Hall for Worshipping Ancestors and more residences for court ladies.

In both the Ming and Qing dynasties there were few buildings specially dedicated to government administration. The central imperial ministries, or boards, were located to the south of the Gate of Heavenly Peace on either side of what is now Tiananmen Square. In the Ming dynasty, the business of government was conducted in the Outer Court. Officials gathered around 3 a.m. outside the Meridian Gate before proceeding to the Hall of Supreme Harmony for the dawn audience, met by the emperor who had to walk (or be carried) a distance of 500 metres from his chambers in the Palace of Heavenly Purity (*Qianqing Gong*) in the Inner Court to the north. Towards the end of the Ming, however, the strict system of daily audiences broke down. The Wanli Emperor ('broad vision', r. 1572–1620), who had a running dispute with his officials over who would succeed him, dispensed with such audiences altogether for over two decades. He relied instead on the services of the palace eunuchs in dealing with his ministers. During that time, his equally tenacious officials carried on the business of empire regardless. They gathered in the tenebrous light to bow ritually to the emperor's empty throne, whereupon they returned to the weighty tasks of empire.

Some trace the rot in the system as far back as 1426, a few years after the Forbidden City was built. In direct contravention of the first Ming emperor's order that eunuchs be kept illiterate and away from power, the Xuande Emperor ('proclaimed virtue', r. 1426–35) established the Internal School (*Nei Shutang*) for palace eunuchs. Once they learned to read and write and were able to perform minor secretarial tasks, the ascendancy of the eunuchs proved to be unstoppable. By the late Ming, the Forbidden City is said to have had in its employ more than 100,000 eunuchs of various ranks, who became enmeshed in every aspect of court life.

Emperors used the eunuchs as a counterbalance to the civil officials, but over time they came to form a shadow bureaucracy that worked in parallel and often against the scholar officials. Although there were 'good eunuchs' who helped educate rulers in the ways of virtue and responsibility, the late Ming dynasty saw at different times the rise of four notorious 'eunuch dictators' who, through their control over various emperors, the secret service and the eunuch bureaucracy effectively held sway over the empire. The extent of the advantages such a chief eunuch could enjoy was evident when the rapaciously corrupt Liu Jin fell from grace in 1510. Apart from an extensive mansion, Liu had amassed a personal fortune of 2.5 million taels in gold and silver, two suits of solid gold armour, twenty-five pounds of precious stones, 3,000 gold rings and brooches, 500 gold plates and over 4,000 gem-studded belts. Eunuchs were, however, essential for the running of the Forbidden City. They performed every service in the palace, from the most menial tasks as cleaners and gardeners (tending to the numerous potted plants that often filled the terraces and courtyards of the imperial dwellings) and as entertainers, to their most important role as messengers and even as unofficial advisers. In the case of the imperial progeny they were playmates, confidants and even instructors in sex education.

The Outer Court was a place of expansive courtyards dominated by imposing halls built on marble 'Mount Sumeru stages'. The Inner Court, by contrast, was a warren of narrower walled passageways with entrances debouching into more intimate courtyards. Apart from the numerous residences of the emperor's wives, consorts, concubines and women relatives, there were kitchens, tearooms, studios, libraries, storerooms and the cramped dwellings of the numerous eunuch servants who ran the day-to-day life of the court. Indeed, intimacy and intrigue rather than vistas, distance and spectacle reflected the spatial and social differences between the rear palaces and the anterior halls. The Three Palaces of the Inner Court mirrored on a smaller and more intimate scale the grandeur and hierarchical ordering of the Three Halls of the Outer Court.

The original Palace of Heavenly Purity, built in 1420 as the sleeping and living quarters of the Ming emperors, burned to the ground when a display of pyrotechnics went awry in 1514. It was soon rebuilt. The emperor hosted New Year's banquets for officials in this palace. As almost all of the Ming emperors died here, it was also the site for imperial funerals, its side rooms used by the deceased emperor's mourning offspring. Thirteen Ming emperors made this palace their home. Nine chambers on its upper and lower floors were sealed off to provide warmth in winter; between them they contained seventy-seven *kang* – sleeping platforms that could be internally heated. The arrangement provided the rulers with a degree of privacy, if not security, as the Jiajing Emperor ('vast serenity', r. 1522–67), a devotee of sexual cruelty and elixirs of immortality, learned to his grief. From a young age he was known for being particularly sadistic towards palace women whom he used for both physical satisfaction and in his pursuit of the elixir. Finally, in the early hours of 27 November 1542,

11. The Palace of Heavenly Purity in the 1920s with eunuchs carrying a palanquin. The abdicated Xuantong Emperor Puyi still celebrated Lunar New Year and his birthday in this palace.

more than a dozen young women from the seraglio invaded his bedchamber, tied him down by his arms and legs, but failed in their attempts to strangle him. The empress raised the alarm when she heard the struggling and the emperor was rescued. Sixteen women implicated in what was to all intents and purposes an assassination plot were condemned to die by the excruciating and protracted punishment known as 'death by a thousand cuts' (*lingchi*). Not that Jiajing entirely lacked warmth. He was known for his love of cats, so much so that he would ignore calls to attend court so that he could play with his favourites, Snow Brow and Tiger. Snow Brow was given the title of 'Dragon' and when it died enjoyed a formal burial and a tomb on Prospect Hill behind the palace (the tomb was destroyed in the 1960s). Tiger was interred in a golden casket. However, after recovering from his near-death experience at the hands of his palace women, Jiajing fled the Forbidden City and lived thereafter in the West Gardens (*Xi Yuan*) (now the Lake Palaces), never daring to return to the Palace of Heavenly Purity.

Behind the Palace of Heavenly Purity, the small square Hall of Union (*Jiaotai Dian*) replicated the position and dimensions of the Hall of Central Harmony in the Outer Court. It was intended as the empress's throne room, though from the time of the Qianlong Emperor onwards it was used to house the royal seals. A large plaque bearing two characters written in the hand of the Kangxi Emperor reads 'Inaction' (*wu wei*), the ancient Taoist notion of ideal government. Such calligraphic inscriptions appear in many palace buildings, exhorting the ruler to govern well and wisely. The hall also contains an exquisite example of the elaborate caisson ceilings which feature in many of the Forbidden City's major buildings. During the Qing dynasty, the emperor would formally receive the empress in this hall. The palace ladies also gathered in the court of this building for the initial rites of the imperial sericulture ceremonies.

The last of the Three Rear Palaces is the Palace of Earthly Tranquillity (*Kunning Gong*). The palace that stood on this site in the Ming dynasty burned to the ground twice; during the Qing it was rebuilt in 1645 and again in 1798, after being destroyed in a conflagration the previous year. During the Ming dynasty, it had been the empress's quarters, but in 1645 the Manchus consecrated the building to their ancient shamanistic beliefs. The Qianlong and subsequent emperors were married here. The quivers, bows, drums and boar-roasting pits in this palace, all of which featured in religious ceremonies that involved dancing and ritual slaughter, are the trappings of the royal clan's private faith (see chapter 4).

Private life and the complex play between power and intrigue, as concubines conspired to produce an heir for the emperor, was focused in two small courtyards on the western flank of the Three Rear Palaces – the Hall of Mental Cultivation (*Yangxin Dian*) and the Palace of Terrestrial Assistance (*Yikun Gong*). The latter, with its ornate interior decoration, at its entrance features two cranes symbolising longevity, similar to those of the Hall of Supreme Harmony. They date from the time of Cixi, the Dowager Empress whose rise to power shaped the last half-century of the Forbidden City's imperial history (see chapter 5).

The relatively unassuming Hall of Mental Cultivation, originally intended as a place for the emperor to rest but later used as a dwelling, during the Qing dynasty became the most important building in the Forbidden City. The

Shunzhi Emperor ('favourable sway', r. 1644–61) had lived there occasionally and finally died there, but it came to be used as a residential office and design studio by the Kangxi and Yongzheng ('concord and rectitude', r. 1725–35) emperors who directed the work of both the government and the palace workshops from there (see chapter 3). Yongzheng located his Office of Military Intelligence (*Junji Chu*), the imperial 'war cabinet', immediately south of the Hall of Mental Cultivation. The network of discreet alleys connecting the hall with the women's quarters and the offices of the highest officials afforded its residents a certain degree of privacy, but it also provided the perfect architectural cover for palace schemes.

A small compound, the Hall of Mental Cultivation could only be entered through three gates. In its northern wall there were two gates; the western of these was called the Gate of Fulfilment (*Ruyi Men*), while the eastern was known as the Gate of Good Auspices (*Jixiang Men*). The Gate of Fulfilment led directly to the quarters of the Dowager Empress, but the north-east entry afforded passage to the apartments of a concubine or wife away from the gaze of the Dowager Empress during the long years of her occupancy in the nineteenth century. For this reason the north-eastern passage was also dubbed the Gate of the Male Mantis (*Zhongsi Men*), a reverential reference to the legendary fertility of the praying mantis which only needed to rustle its wings to attract female mantises, each of which was then reputed to give birth to ninety-nine offspring. The third gate gave access to the south-east corner of the compound into the Hall of Mental Cultivation; from the time of Yongzheng, this was the entrance by which the emperor's close advisers in the Office of Military Intelligence entered, as did head artisans from the various

12. Exterior view of the Hall of Mental Cultivation, 1922. This picture of the emperor's main residence in the Forbidden City was taken during the era of Puyi's 'little court' (1912–1924) that followed the abdication of the Qing dynasty. Pots of flowers were amassed in the otherwise stark courtyards of the Inner Court. The Manchus were also renowned for keeping birds, goldfish and crickets. In the later years of the Qing dynasty, dogs also found favour as pets with court ladies, in particular the Empress Dowager.

workshops. The Hall of Mental Cultivation thus became the centre of power – and plots – in the palace.

Apart from ceremonial, ritual and residential halls, workshops, kitchens and buildings individually devoted to the sustenance of the intellectual and physical lives of the emperors, their extensive families and the state itself, the sacred grounds of the Forbidden City were also filled with shrines and temples dedicated to the many religions the emperors supported. It also contained theatres and gardens, complete with belvederes, pavilions and vistas. To the north of the Three Rear Palaces was the Taoist temple known as the Hall of Imperial Peace (*Qin'an Dian*), which enshrined a powerful deity and was designed to provide geomantic security to the whole complex.

Around the temple the Qianlong Emperor laid out a southern-Chinese-style garden, the Imperial Garden (*Yu Huayuan*) featuring elaborate rockeries, imitation hills (*jia shan*), kiosks and pavilions. It was bound on its south side by the Gate of Heavenly Unity (*Tianyi Men*) and on its north by the Gate of Accord with the True (*Shunzhen Men*). This garden was a unique concession to frivolity along the south–north axis of power that ran from the Meridian Gate at the southern entrance through to the Gate of Divine Prowess (*Shenwu Men*) in the north. Here, at this northernmost point, the palace servants would enter and leave the Forbidden City (it is now the other main entrance to the Palace Museum).

Ringing the entire complex were crenellated walls set with elaborate multi-storey watchtowers at each corner further protected by a moat over fifty metres wide and four metres deep. The moat was never assailed by invaders; the battlements and gates always proved the easier breach.

3

RISE AND DECLINE

Although the Forbidden City we see today is largely a construction of the 'invasion dynasty' of the Qing, its architecture is generally faithful to Ming style, even its rebuilt structures conforming to the older codes of design and decoration. The Manchu rulers of the Qing – themselves the leaders of a coalition of powerful clans and ethnic groups – were assiduous in retaining and enhancing aspects of Han Chinese culture and practice from the Ming era. They were also anxious that their rule, and moral sway, over the vast territory of China be accepted. Like China itself, the Forbidden City enjoyed its most impressive and prosperous period in the late seventeenth and eighteenth centuries, during the well-documented reigns of three Manchu emperors – Kangxi, his son Yongzheng and his grandson Qianlong.

The Chinese empire would reach its apogee under these celebrated rulers, men who excelled in dominating the empire, expanding its borders and creating a multi-ethnic domain that in many ways is still reflected in China today. The three emperors brought a very different style of rule to the Forbidden City but, like all competent heirs to the Chinese dynastic system, they would be exercised by the need to govern well and ensure the stability of the imperial family and the succession to the throne.

The Forbidden City was not, however, the three emperors' favoured abode; it was too labyrinthine and circumscribing for their taste, its ingrained habits of management were too oppressive. But its palaces housed the offices in which they consulted and directed their senior officials and, as mentioned in the last chapter, the Hall of Mental Cultivation effectively became the centre of the emperors' working lives, and therefore the centre of the Qing empire itself. It was also the hub of a geographically extensive network of palaces and courts administered by the Imperial Household Department, the élite Qing institution that – in place of the eunuchs of the Ming dynasty – co-ordinated the running of the Inner Court on the emperor's behalf.

Kangxi's predecessor, the Shunzhi Emperor, had followed Ming custom by officially residing in the Palace of Heavenly Purity, although he preferred the Hall of Mental Cultivation. Living there he found time to spend with his favourite concubine, Dong E, who was despised by his dominating mother, the Xiaozhuang Empress, a Mongol noblewoman originally by the name of Borjit Bumbutai. Xiaozhuang may have been a Mongol but she was cast in the same iron mould as Manchu imperial mothers and grandmothers, who stereotypically attempted to control their sons and grandsons as well as the imperial succession.

When Dong E died of smallpox, following debilitating post-natal complications, Shunzhi was inconsolable. His attendants had to maintain a vigil in order to ensure that he did not commit suicide. The emperor's interest in Buddhism increased with his grief and he took a vow of celibacy, enraging his mother. Her fury was further inflamed by the possibility that he would abdicate and become a monk but, within three months of Dong E's death, Shunzhi himself fell victim to smallpox. The Manchus considered the Forbidden City and Beijing in general, with its low elevation and climatic extremes, a place of miasma and plague. On 4 February 1661, the emperor summoned two of his grand secretaries to the Hall of Mental Cultivation to draft his will. They arrived there in the dead of night, and worked through the following day until the third and final version met with his approval. Although there would be persistent rumours that Shunzhi had left the Forbidden City by stealth to become an itinerant Buddhist monk, it is almost certain that he succumbed to the ravaging disease the day after he completed his will.

In 1662, Shunzhi's son and designated heir, Xuanye, ascended the throne as the Kangxi ('lasting prosperity') Emperor. He was not yet seven. Kangxi lived and studied in the Hall of Mental Cultivation. The Manchus regarded his vigil there to be the appropriate form of mourning and respect for his father, whose body was removed to the Palace of Heavenly Purity in preparation for burial. The Shunzhi Emperor was the last Qing ruler to be cremated, a practice that the Manchus abandoned as they increasingly accepted Han Chinese funerary rituals involving the embalming and interment of the dead. His ashes were none the less buried with great ceremony in the first of the new dynastic mausolea at the Eastern Qing Tombs (*Qing Dong Ling*) in Zunhua county, Hebei province.

Four Manchu regents effectively governed for the young emperor until 1669, when, with the help of his uncle, Songgotu, Kangxi seized the reins of government from the dominant regent, Oboi, and assumed full power. The Manchus had inherited some of the Ming institutions of government, including the Grand Secretariat (*Nei Ge*), nominally the highest decision-making body located in the Outer Court, but its power was taken over by the Manchu Council of Adviser Princes (*Yizheng Wangdachen Huiyi*). When Kangxi gained power, he drew his closest advisers not only from the most prominent Manchu clans active in the Inner Court but also from Han Chinese officials. In 1677, in order to circumvent the interfering Manchu families he set up his own advisory body, the Southern Study (*Nan Shufang*). Its name was derived from its location in the south-west corner of the Palace of Heavenly Purity.

Kangxi's advisers travelled with him wherever he went. As he grew older, his horizons expanded and he increasingly admitted to his inner circle ethnic Han Chinese intimates, including Gao Shiqi, who was widely esteemed for his calligraphy, poetry and erudition. The emperor remained ever wary of the intrigues of the Manchu élite, who sought to ally themselves with any potential heir to the throne. In 1703, acting on information supplied by Gao Shiqi, Kangxi had his original mentor Songgotu incarcerated, whereupon he was 'permitted to die'. One of the ostensible reasons for this murder was that his old mentor had been complicit in the debauchery of the son that Kangxi had originally designated as heir apparent.

Palace intrigues surrounding the succession to the throne focused on the Inner Court and its apartments. The politics of choosing an heir apparent were fraught. Naturally, there was much competition among palace women to produce an heir. The mechanics by which the emperor selected his companion for the night (or longer) from among his many wives, consorts and concubines of varying rank has, not surprisingly, been the

13. 'Portrait of the Kangxi Emperor in Informal Dress at His Writing Table',
scroll painting, anon.

subject of much florid speculation. There is, however, little reliable documentation. The arrangements for the nocturnal rendezvous seem to have been the province of the Office of Respectful Service (*Jingshi Fang*), an agency of the Imperial Household Department. It is only in works of fictive history known in Chinese as 'history from the wilds' (*yeshi*), or apocryphal accounts, that we find recorded the alleged details of its operations. Two entries in the early Republican collection *Apocryphal Histories of the Qing Palace* describe how the emperor would choose from 'menu cards' (*shanpai*) bearing the names of his palace women. The cards were presented to him on a silver tray at the end of his meal by a eunuch from the Office of Respectful Service and the emperor would place the card of the selected lady face down. Under the direction of the Chief of the Imperial Bedchamber eunuchs delivered the chosen one to the emperor's bed in the Hall of Mental Cultivation wrapped in a silken carpet but naked, and therefore unable to conceal any weapon on her person. Once the emperor had retired in readiness, they deftly introduced her through a gap between the quilts at the foot of the bed. A director of the Office, accompanied by a burly porter – naturally also a eunuch – would stand outside the emperor's window and call out 'Time's up!' (*Shi shihou le!*) when he believed that adequate congress had been achieved. The consort or concubine was removed in the reverse manner to her delivery, and the director would ask the emperor whether she should be allowed to conceive. If the reply was in the negative, then they would drain the 'dragon seed' from her vaginal passage; if the emperor answered in the affirmative a written record would be kept of the encounter.

The palace regulations governing this system were said to

have been based on Ming precedents, adopted by the Shunzhi Emperor to curb the uncontrolled consequences of the 'sexual dissipation' (*yinyi*) of his descendants. But Shunzhi's own love for Dong E clearly flouted these self same rules. At the time he adopted them, his son was too young for 'sexual dissipation' to have been a concern. It is possible, then, that this unconventional mode of delivering a woman to the emperor for the night might have been a ploy to hoodwink an interfering mother.

These anecdotes, however colourful, contradict others recounting palace household regulations, presumably policed by the Office of Respectful Service, which decreed that empresses and concubines could sleep with the emperor only in designated bedrooms in the Hall of Mental Cultivation, or in other specified palaces within the Forbidden City. The *kang* in the eastern closet bedroom of the hall was always prepared in readiness for the empress; that in the western bedroom for a consort or concubine. In order to avoid assassination, the bedcovers in all the bedrooms were removed at the end of the night, so that no one knew where and with whom (if anyone) the emperor had slept. In the late nineteenth century, the Guangxu Emperor ('glorious succession', r. 1875–1908) would have the beds in both bedchambers mussed up so that his adoptive mother the Empress Dowager Cixi could not discover whether or not he had slept with the consort whom he loved and she despised (see chapter 5).

By the nineteenth century, as the Manchu emperors produced far fewer sons than in the past, the person of the empress dowager (*huang taihou*, the imperial mother) assumed an importance only ever witnessed in the powerful women of earlier dynasties, and much like that of their

Ottoman equivalents. Unlike his Ottoman contemporaries, though, a designated Manchu heir did not necessarily embark on a rampage of fratricide to ensure his succession. The Yongzheng Emperor did, however, incarcerate most of his brothers after assuming the throne following the death of his father Kangxi in 1722.

For emperor, empress dowager, empress, consort and concubine alike, the stakes were high. Success and security were measured by the production of a malleable male heir to the throne. Not surprisingly, the themes of fertility and the production of sons were reiterated throughout the Forbidden City, and the palaces were decorated with peaches, cranes, bats and persimmons, to name only some of the multitude of motifs that signified longevity, fecundity, harmony and happiness.

Having consolidated his control over China Proper, the main territory of the Ming dynasty, in 1684 Kangxi revived the ancient practice of southern expeditions or 'imperial tours of the south' (*nan xun*). It was a tradition dating back to the powerful First Emperor of the Qin dynasty, Qin Shihuang (r. 221–10 BCE). Each southern expedition afforded the Manchu emperor, who after all was the head of a dynasty that had violently conquered the Han Chinese people, the opportunity to dazzle his southern subjects, as well as to introduce himself and learn about their concerns and needs. Hydrology projects, water management and local governance, which were all crucial to the effective rule over the vast agrarian economy of China and the supply of goods to the north, were also crucial aspects of these tours of inspection. Kangxi travelled in the company of his mother, the dowager empress, and this suffused his journeys with the glow of Confucian filial piety. He undertook six such trips, each lasting approximately three months. These progresses through the provinces brought the emperor into direct contact with Han Chinese culture as opposed to the Manchu culture with which he was surrounded at the palace. Moreover, they demonstrated to the literati of the south, from whose number the majority of administrators of the empire were selected, that the emperor was worthy of the cultural world over which he held sway. These travels also inspired the emperor to introduce some of the architectural and landscaping elegance of the south to the imperial environment of the north, particularly in the extensive garden palaces north-west of Beijing and at the Imperial Mountain Lodge (*Bishu Shanzhuang*) at Chengde (also known as Rehe or Jehol), beyond the Great Wall in today's Hebei province. By taking his Inner Court with him from the Forbidden City to the hunting grounds in the north-east, as well as to Chengde and to the garden palaces he had begun building in north-west Beijing and even to southern China on his tours, Kangxi achieved his goal of maintaining a mobile court at the centre of a dynamically expanding empire.

In 1686, Kangxi embarked on an ambitious palace-building programme in the Eastern and Western Six Palaces (*Dong Liu Gong* and *Xi Liu Gong* respectively) of the Forbidden City. Most of the buildings which we see there today are not the originals constructed by Kangxi, and the purposes of many of them have changed over time. The Qianlong Emperor rebuilt a number of them in the latter half of the eighteenth century. Kangxi's Palace of Prolonged Happiness (*Yanxi Gong*), however, is one of the most exotic structures within the entire Forbidden City and a dramatic example of the architectural changes made in the palace over the last two centuries. Located in the Eastern Six Palaces behind the Hall for Worshipping Ancestors, the Palace of Prolonged Happiness served as a home for imperial concubines until it burned to the ground in 1845. (The Empress Dowager Longyu, the surviving wife of the Guangxu Emperor, had it rebuilt in 1909. She additionally authorised the construction of a fanciful three-storey Western-style building popularly known as the Crystal Palace (*Shuijing Gong*) which is surrounded by a moat that was supposed to be filled with water from the abundant springs at Jade Source Mountain (*Yuquan Shan*) in Beijing's north-west. This complex remained incomplete due to a lack of funds and was partially damaged in a bombing raid in 1917 during a failed attempt to restore the monarchy. Since 2005, the two-storey side halls have housed exhibitions and research centres related to ceramics and traditional painting.)

Of the Eastern and Western Six Palaces that Kangxi built to house the imperial seraglio, the Palace of Eternal Harmony (*Yonghe Gong*) to the immediate north of the Water Hall reportedly preserves most faithfully early Ming architectural style in its arrangement of courtyards and buildings. Here Kangxi rebuilt what had been a Ming palace for concubines as the residence of his secondary consort, best known by her posthumous title of Empress Dowager Xiaogong Ren, the mother of his successor Yinzhen, the Yongzheng Emperor. Kangxi also built extensively in the south-east precincts of the Forbidden City: in 1683 he undertook the construction of the Hall of Literary Flourishing and to its east the Hall of Relaying the Mind (*Chuanxin Dian*). As a centre of scholarship, the Hall of Literary Flourishing became one of the most important palaces in the eastern precinct, and the pursuit of scholarship would remain a focus of Kangxi's life. As a child he was educated in written Manchu, his first language, as well as in Chinese and in the martial arts of the Manchus, archery and horsemanship, which prepared him for hunting and warfare – both pursuits in which he excelled. He also kept hunting dogs both in the Forbidden City and at the Imperial Mountain Lodge (his grandson, the Qianlong Emperor, would have portraits made of his favourite dogs). He was also fascinated by science. The death of his father the emperor Shunzhi from smallpox vindicated the deep-seated Manchu fear of the disease; Kangxi would maintain a lifelong interest in combating it. He introduced inoculation against smallpox, which involved inhaling the sloughed off skin from dried smallpox pustules, to his troops and children. When he was forty, Kangxi himself contracted malaria and, so the story goes, only the quinine given to him by the Western missionary doctors at court saved him, despite his initial wariness: 'I had the quinine that the Westerners brought tested on outsiders and then on members of the imperial clan before I took it for myself.' Nevertheless, the experience prompted the emperor to set up a small Western medical laboratory adjacent to his apartments at the Hall of Mental Cultivation. He also directed his physicians to pay attention to the study of anatomy, the dissection of a bear being the recorded legacy of this endeavour.

Medicine aside, the Jesuit missionaries who served at the Chinese court from the late Ming dynasty boasted an array of technical skills that Kangxi wanted to put to full use. This international, and often entrepreneurial, band of missionaries envisaged their poorly rewarded work as foreign experts as the first step towards the conversion of the empire through the person of the emperor. This proved more elusive than it had been during the Ming dynasty, when high-level conversions were more frequent. Kangxi was none the less impressed by the Jesuits' astronomical, mathematical, mechanical, medical, mapping and musical skills. When working with one of them, Jean-François Gerbillon, on various projects, Kangxi gave him his father Shunzhi's bedchamber in the Hall of Mental Cultivation.

Gerbillon had been sent to serve the Kangxi Emperor as a mathematician. In addition to translating mathematical treatises into Manchu, he helped translate into Latin the 1689 Treaty of Nerchinsk with Russia and served as a cartographer for the expanding Qing empire. He has left a detailed account of the layout of the Hall of Mental Cultivation in his diary entry of 16 January 1690. The central hall, he noted, was 'neither splendid nor majestic' and 'was furnished simply'; at its centre was a raised dais covered with 'several Turcoman rugs of the type we use, but these were very ordinary and decorated with dragons'. A gilded timber chair was set towards the centre of the dais; Gerbillon was unimpressed by the striking *plafond* ceiling with its intricately carved dragon panels and the caisson from which a large shining sphere, emblematic of the pearl of wisdom, was suspended. The eastern side room, where the emperor rested, was unpainted and its walls coated with white paper. There were no curtains. A *kang* – effectively the emperor's throne in this room – ran along one wall, overlaid with white felt rugs, with a large black satin cushion at its centre and another pillow on which he could recline. On the *kang* there were also several small tables, which held books and inkstones, and an ancient bronze brazier. In the room, the emperor had placed the wax

14. Interior of the audience chamber in the Hall of Mental Cultivation showing the *plafond* ceiling.

fruit presented as a gift by Gerbillon and his party when they arrived in Beijing, and to one side was a display case containing small agate cups, walnuts and other curios fashioned from amber, as well as bibelots made from white jade and set with rubies and other gems. An extremely ornate yellow silk casket contained an array of imperial seals of varying sizes made of agate, white jade, nephrite and crystal. Gerbillon was clearly already applying himself to his Manchu lessons, recording with obvious satisfaction Kangxi's aside that his pronunciation was 'accurate' and listing the meanings of some inscriptions in 'Tartar script'. He also noted that a section of one room in the Hall of Mental Cultivation was filled with 'the most exquisitely detailed models of objects in paper' fashioned by the emperor's artisans.

In 1722, the sixty-first year of his reign, the Kangxi Emperor died at the Garden of Delightful Spring (*Changchun Yuan*), a palace north-west of Beijing where he spent much of the year. (It was destroyed in 1860 by an Anglo-French army that invaded following the disastrous Second Opium War and peace negotiations that were bungled by the Manchu court. It is now the site of student and staff dormitories belonging to Peking University.) Many believe Yinzhen (later the Yongzheng Emperor) altered his father's will so that it designated him, the fourth son, heir over the favoured fourteenth son, Yunti, his brother by the same mother. The evidence is circumstantial. His critics maintain, for example, that Yongzheng peremptorily abandoned the Palace of Heavenly Purity, his father's formal residence, to live in the Hall of Mental Cultivation. However, as successor and chief mourner, it was his obligation to do so during the 27-day mourning period. Other alleged evidence of irregular

15. The Yongzheng Emperor in Western dress and wig from 'An Album of Yongzheng at Leisure', one of thirteen leaves, anon.

behaviour prompted by guilt was Yongzheng's decision to be buried in a mausoleum far from his father. His tomb, in what would become known as the Western Qing Tombs (*Qing Xi Ling*), was hundreds of kilometres from that of Kangxi, who like his father the Shunzhi Emperor was buried in the geomantically auspicious and physically majestic Eastern Qing Tombs. This decision was interpreted as an attempt to avoid the torment his father's ghost would inflict on his unfilial soul. And yet it is documented that when he fell ill Kangxi delegated Yinzhen to conduct ceremonies in his stead at the Altar of Heaven (*Tian Tan*), a clear indication that he was indeed the chosen successor.

The reign of the Yongzheng Emperor, which began in 1723, marked a shift towards more secretive and dictatorial government. As a prince Yinzhen had showed himself to be a person of great refinement, the Garden of Perfect Brightness (*Yuanming Yuan*) just north of Kangxi's Garden of Delightful Spring, being a monument to his imagination and style. Numerous pavilions and studios – many of which were inspired by lines of poetry or lyrical fancy – were scattered in a vast manmade landscape of hillocks, lakes and streams. As emperor he would remove the court there and effectively run the empire from this garden demesne. His princely mansion in Beijing also shows the scale of his ambition. It is now the Yonghe Gong lama temple in the north-east of the Inner City (*Nei Cheng*) of old Beijing. However, as a ruler Yongzheng's paranoia and obsession with secrecy are well documented. These and his preoccupation with image and popularity have only fed speculation that he had in fact stolen the throne. For instance, he alarmed his contemporaries and raised their suspicions when, on assuming power, he issued an edict demanding that all memorials and edicts bearing the comments of the Kangxi Emperor in imperial vermilion ink were to be handed over to the central government, and that anyone who failed to do so would be punished severely. Whatever the legitimacy of his own claim to the throne, Yongzheng introduced a new, simple system for designating his own heir apparent. He kept one copy of the name of the heir on his person, and concealed the other in a small casket behind the plaque above the throne in the Palace of Heavenly Purity. Only at the time of the emperor's death would the contents of the two documents be compared and the heir announced.

In the first year of his reign, the Yongzheng Emperor set up the Advisory Council Office (*Yizheng Chu*) inside the Forbidden City. He required the Grand Secretariat, the formal instrument of government, to defer to them in all matters. Although the Grand Secretariat continued to exist in name, thereby placating its supporters among the Manchu princes, Yongzheng was determined to override it. The new emperor reviewed memorials sent to him in the Western Heated Chamber (*Xi Nuange*) (a 'heated chamber' being a partitioned alcove within a larger room with a closet bed consisting of a heated and raised *kang* bed built along one side) in the Hall of Mental Cultivation. In it hangs a couplet in Yongzheng's own hand which encapsulates his political philosophy and expresses the urgency that Yongzheng brought to the task of concentrating all power in his own hands: 'Only if one man rules the world can the world uphold that one man' (*Wei yi yiren zhi tianxia, qi wei tianxia feng yiren*). The resumption of war with the Mongols along the Qing empire's north-western frontiers in 1730 provided him with an ideal opportunity to consolidate his power.

At the outset of the war the Grand Secretariat was responsible for handling military intelligence. As it was located in the vicinity of the Hall of Literary Flourishing in the southeast of the Forbidden City, far from the Inner Court and Yongzheng's study in the Hall of Mental Cultivation, there were many opportunities for security breaches. Therefore, in 1733, the emperor set up a new body called the Office of Military Intelligence, locating it in a row of small offices on the north-west side of the square of the Gate of Heavenly Purity. Although a wall separated the offices from the emperor's kitchens (*Yushan Fang*) on the southern perimeter of the Hall of Mental Cultivation, a narrow passage less than two metres in width and just short of fifty metres long connected it with the hall. The emperor could thus secretly summon his top officials at any time. Yongzheng also introduced a system of secret memorials whereby communications to the emperor did not pass through the usual chain of scrutinising officials but were directly relayed to him in a sealed casket; only the emperor and the original correspondent had the key to open the casket. The throne's replies were conveyed by the same means. This system of secret memorials created an atmosphere which facilitated abuses of power. The imperial bureaucracy was gradually paralysed by caution while a second, shadow bureaucracy of officials reporting directly to the emperor actually ran the empire.

Yongzheng is reviled to this day in works of popular culture. During his reign he personally visited ruin upon many prominent families associated with other princely claimants to the throne, among them the Cao family, who had previously been favourites of his father Kangxi. Cao Yin had been Kangxi's personal confidant and his mother had been Kangxi's wet nurse. Although Cao Yin amassed great wealth, his grandson, Cao Xueqin, was reduced to living in abject poverty on the outskirts of Beijing, where in the mid eighteenth century he wrote the greatest and most abidingly popular work of Chinese fiction, *The Dream of the Red Chamber* (*Honglou Meng*), also known as *The Story of the Stone*. The novel is a veritable encyclopaedia of late traditional Chinese life and culture, as well as being a beguiling story of predestination, love, wealth and stately decline. It recreates in loving detail a final synthesis of Han Chinese and Manchu high culture as it existed in the mid eighteenth century. Although they were ethnically Han Chinese, the Cao family had been accorded Manchu status and lived according to Manchu mores. Their womenfolk wore elaborate Manchu headdresses and did not bind their feet. The author may have written 'with reminders of his poverty around him', but many of his close friends were princelings and members of the imperial clan. In many ways, the aristocratic world portrayed in his novel, the sensibilities of its characters, the daily ritual of their lives, are those that would have been found on a far grander scale in the Inner Court of the Forbidden City at the time.

When confronted by anti-Manchu sentiment, which was widespread following their bloody conquest of China, Yongzheng proved a spirited and magnanimous defender of the Manchus and their right to rule. But despite the odium attached to his harsh treatment of the Cao family and others, he was none the less an extremely competent administrator and diligent in the pursuit of his duties; a number of his innovations ensured that the Qing remained powerful. He also spent considerable time and resources expanding the garden palace bestowed on him by his father, the Garden of Perfect

Brightness. (It was destroyed by the same Anglo-French forces that razed his father's garden palace. It is now China's 'national ruin', a park that symbolises the country's humiliation in the nineteenth century.) He also undertook new construction work in the Forbidden City. In 1726, he built the Temple of the City God in its north-west corner (see chapter 1), the Archery Pavilion in 1730, the Palace of Fasting (*Zhai Gong*) one year later, and in 1735 he constructed the Palace of Longevity and Health on the western side of the Palace of Benevolent Tranquillity (see chapter 6 for the fate of the contents of this palace).

Ironically, in the very same year that the Palace of Longevity and Health was being built, Yongzheng died suddenly, at the age of fifty-seven, most probably from a combination of overwork and indulgence in lead-based elixirs, part of his search for eternal life. The throne passed to his fourth son, Hongli, who had been the favourite grandson of Kangxi and Kangxi's widow and whom he had groomed for the role of emperor. The reign of Yongzheng had been prosperous and characterised by wise economic management. That of Hongli, the Qianlong Emperor, would see unprecedented abundance and munificence, but there seemed to be no rein on the imperial purse. Qianlong was as extravagant as Yongzheng had been cautious. At great expense, he continued the wars in Turkestan and eventually oversaw the extension of the Qing empire deep into Central Asia.

Qianlong's earnest display of the trappings of filial piety was immortalised in the painting 'Spring's Peaceful Messenger' (*Ping'an Chunxin Tu*) by Giuseppe Castiglione, one of the Jesuits serving in his court as an artisan or artist. The painting, which depicts Yongzheng conferring a spray of apricot

16. 'Spring's Peaceful Messenger' by Giuseppe Castiglione showing theYongzheng Emperor with Hongli, the future Qianlong Emperor.

blossom on his son, signifies the legitimacy of the succession and remained fixed to a wall in the Hall of Mental Cultivation for several decades. However, in true Manchu tradition, Qianlong's overriding filial devotion was to his mother. She accompanied him on four of his six famous southern tours (in 1751, 1757, 1762 and 1765), on three of his five pilgrimages to the Buddhist temple complexes at Wutai Mountain in Shanxi province (in 1746, 1750 and 1761), and on three of the five pilgrimages to the Confucian Temple in Shandong (in 1748, 1771 and 1776), completing the last when she was eighty-four. Qianlong spent much of his childhood with his mother in what were called the *Qianxi Ersuo* courtyards of the inner western precinct of the Inner Court, far from his father, who was often ensconced in the Garden of Perfect Brightness. In later life, Qianlong remodelled the *Qianxi Ersuo* area within the Double Brilliance Gate (*Chonghua Men*) as the Hall of Adoration (*Chongjing Dian*), the Palace of Double Brilliance (*Chonghua Gong*) and the Azure Cloud Hall (*Cuiyun Guan*), and he would often entertain his courtiers here (see chapter 4). The buildings never served again as the residence of an heir apparent.

Qianlong's southern expeditions dwarfed those of his grandfather in scale and frequency. They also gave rise to a body of popular fiction in which the emperor escapes from his retinue and experiences all sorts of adventures *incognito*. As a result of the actual tours, however, Qianlong introduced southern garden landscapes not only to the Forbidden City, but on a far grander scale to the garden palaces in the north-west of Beijing enjoyed by his father and grandfather. He also expanded and embellished these outer palaces. (They were all destroyed in the punitive 1860 Anglo-French campaign mentioned above. Something of their extent and style, however, can be seen in the Summer Palace (*Yihe Yuan*) rebuilt in the late nineteenth century.)

Qianlong remained an emperor on the move, spending most of the year at the garden palaces or the imperial hunting grounds. Yet the Forbidden City was centre stage to his eventful life and vast enterprise. Although he was resident in the Hall of Mental Cultivation for only three months a year on average, the Forbidden City was his starting point and his ultimate destination. For midway through his reign Qianlong turned his energies back to the Forbidden City. He delighted in the pomp and circumstance for which the spectacular palace allowed, giving him the opportunity to display in regal manner the herd of thirty elephants that he kept just inside the Military Display Gate (*Xuanwu Men*) (their pens are now the site of the Xinhua News Agency). Qianlong expended enormous energy and divested a fortune in his efforts to make the palace complex ever more sumptuous and comfortable. He built the first imperial theatre in the Inner Court, sparking a fashion for indoor and outdoor theatres there and at the other palaces. He also lavished attention on the shrines and temples within the Forbidden City. For his retirement, among many other projects in numerous sites around China, he constructed a luxurious 'miniature' of the Forbidden City in its north-east corner (see chapter 5).

Despite a reign of unparalleled grandeur, Qianlong's economic judgement became clouded in the last two decades of his life. His reputation was further sullied by his apparent infatuation with Heshen, a handsome military man rumoured to have been his lover. By dint of imperial favour and the advantages he both surreptitiously and blatantly exacted at court and in the provinces, Heshen became the richest and most powerful man in the empire. Fearful that the royal line would be usurped by Heshen (whose son had been married to the emperor's favourite daughter), many of Qianlong's advisers urged the ageing emperor to promulgate the appointment of his heir apparent.

In 1795, the Qianlong Emperor announced that in order to fulfil his filial obligations and not reign for a period longer than Kangxi's unmatched rule of sixty-one years he would abdicate in the spring of the following year and pass the throne on to his son. He vowed to move out of the Hall of Mental Cultivation and take up residence in his 'mini Forbidden City'. But he never did make the move and, although he stood aside, he retained ultimate power until his death in 1799. He was succeeded by his son, Yongyan, who ruled from the Forbidden City as the Jiaqing Emperor ('vast celebration', r. 1796–1820).

Immediately following his father's death, the new emperor moved against Heshen, accusing him of numerous 'heinous crimes'. These included amassing a personal fortune that was said to be in excess of the royal coffers, and the gross impropriety of copying design features of the Qianlong Emperor's retirement palace in the Forbidden City for the appointment of his private residence. In an act of imperial leniency Heshen was granted leave to commit suicide.

Despite his diligent rule, however, the Jiaqing Emperor could do little to prevent the rapid decline of the empire that he had inherited; the damage that had been inflicted on the country's political and economic systems was too severe. In one remarkable incident resulting from social unrest during his reign, in October 1813 a group of rebels claiming to be members of the Heavenly Principle religious sect that was striving to revive the long-fallen Ming dynasty invaded the Forbidden City itself. Although they were soon overwhelmed and dispatched, their attack on the palace was a sign that the hard-won security and relative social harmony established under the three great emperors were in an increasingly parlous state.

4

A DAY IN THE REIGN

In order to understand Qianlong's Forbidden City better, it may be useful to look at it at the midpoint of his reign. Although his life in the palace had become regularised, it is not possible to use the word routine to characterise the totality of events in that extraordinary maze of courts and walls for even one single day. His own writings, which reflect his activities and rule, are voluminous. Yet, paradoxically, while their detailed content provides an epic chronicle of imperial life, they tend to obscure rather than clarify our understanding of his personality, which is seen on full public display but rarely in private reflection. Qianlong's reign produced a great number of unsubstantiated anecdotes and apocryphal rumours – 'histories from the wilds'. Thus, while we have ample testaments, comments and writings by Qianlong and tens of thousands of official documents from his reign to draw on, the picture that emerges of this most remarkable emperor is tantalisingly less clear than the image we have of his grandfather, Kangxi.

Qianlong's day-to-day activities were recorded in *The Imperial Diary* (*Qiju Zhu*; literally, 'Notes on the Levees and Acts'), a running account detailing the emperor's words and deeds. The diary, however, was more a formalised institution than a record. Already in the sixth century, a Ministry of

Levees and Acts (*Qiju Sheng*) had been established to encompass issues of protocol as well as the recording of the emperor's activities and pronouncements. Later this role was played by various different officials and organisations. Suffice it to say that the office had hoary precedents when its function was revived by the Shunzhi Emperor in 1655. Eight Manchu and Han Chinese officials were appointed to serve in positions combining the duties of protocol master, imperial tutor and diarist. A large part of their duties entailed transcribing copies of edicts and other documents. Their office was located in the western gallery to the south of the Gate of Supreme Harmony, just inside the Meridian Gate and not far from the main throne room. During his reign, Qianlong was served in that office by twenty Manchu and Han Chinese officials.

From the tenth year of Kangxi (1663) to the second year of Xuantong (1910), generations of diarists filled more than 12,000 volumes, producing at least twenty volumes for each year in both Chinese and Manchu. The scholar Wu Shizhou consulted these while also drawing on the archives of the imperial wardrobe, kitchens and provisioners, the *Veritable Records* of the imperial historians, the collections of edicts and writings of Qianlong, the archives of the Grand Secretariat and the Office of Military Intelligence, and a vast array of rigorous scholarship and heterodox sources for his masterful *One Day in the Life of Qianlong* (2006). In this account, Wu provides insights not only into the life of Qianlong but also into the way palace life was regulated by the 'downstairs' attendants.

The staff of the palace comprised a vast army. It is said that there were 100,000 eunuchs in the employ of the palace at the height of 'eunuch power' in the late Ming era. It is hard to imagine this, even if we consider that the part of the Forbidden City that is open to the public today is only one half of the entire complex. A visitor to the palace is struck by the apparent total absence of dining rooms, bathrooms, lavatories, sculleries, kitchens, stables, palace girls' quarters, pantries and workshops which can be seen in any European palace. It is as though all banal and baleful influences have been expunged from the palaces, and only the chrysalis of a former life remains. In reality, many of the areas that housed servants have not been open to the public and many of the amenities, such as the imperial baths and toilets, were modular or transportable.

Wu Shizhou's account of the activities of Qianlong on the eighth day of the first lunar month of the thirtieth year of his reign (28 January 1765) brings the palace back to life and provides an insight into the meticulous and complex management that the running of such an extensive institution must have entailed. On this particular mid-winter's day the emperor woke up in the Hall of Mental Cultivation at 4 a.m. after having retired at 11 p.m. the previous evening. This appears to have been a particularly late night for the emperor, but it was usual for him to rise well before dawn. The imperial levee was not a family event and, unlike European monarchs, Chinese emperors did not hold court in the royal bedchambers. The emperor had slept alone. Eunuch servants removed the lock from the outer gate of the Hall of Mental Cultivation at 4 a.m., and the emperor lit a candle, a signal for the two eunuchs on duty to leap into action. They hurried to the door of the bedchamber and waited expectantly while signalling two others to fetch a pail of hot water from the nearby kitchens and leave it in readiness outside the emperor's door.

As daily attendants of the emperor, they were not required to do the full kowtow that consisted of kneeling and prostrating; instead, they shouted the greeting, 'Good fortune to the Lord of Ten Thousand Years!' (*Wansuiye jixiang!*). This told the other attendants gathered in the alleyway outside the hall that the emperor was descending from his heated *kang* bed. The night's 'curfew' had come to an end. The eunuchs on gate duty began admitting the other servants into the imperial sleeping quarters and the gates of palace courtyards throughout the Forbidden City were opened for the new day.

The chambermaids responsible for the imperial bedding were the first servants to enter the emperor's bedroom. They folded up the quilts and set the gleaming silver pail of hot water for the emperor to wash his face in on a soft cushion of yellow silk embroidered with the dragon motif. Wu tells us that 'the emperor had stopped going to the ablutions room on the western side of his bedroom in recent years', preferring to wash in his bedroom. After he washed his face, the eunuch responsible for brushing his hair and shaving him entered the room, carrying on his head his implements tied up in a yellow silk bundle also embroidered with dragons, soaring through the clouds. He genuflected, removed the bundle from his head and greeting the emperor, opened it. The emperor's long hair was brushed daily and braided into a queue, then his whiskers were trimmed and, every ten days, his frontal scalp was completely shaved in accordance with Manchu custom. Meanwhile, the maids in charge of the bedding and the curtains completed their tasks and withdrew. The room outside the emperor's bedroom was both changing room and imperial ablutions chamber, where a portable commode would have been arranged for the ruler's use. Here, too, the eunuchs waited with the garments and boots selected for the emperor to wear that day.

The *Ledger of Attire* tells us that on this day the emperor wore a small black sable trim hat, a yellow *kesi* ('silk patchwork') gown and a small cape with sable fur trim. The gown itself was also trimmed with sable fur and grey shank fur. He wore white velvet socks, thick white trousers of *chunchou* ('spring silk', a cloth with geometric patterns from Hangzhou), and the whole ensemble was set off with black boots edged with green satin and lined with sheep's wool. At his waist he wore an articulated belt made of panels of emeralds (known in Chinese as *zumulü* from the Arabic *zumurud*) from which pearls were suspended. The emperor dressed himself, unlike at many European courts, where the monarch simply positioned himself for the royal dressers. Outside a heated palanquin carried by four eunuchs was positioned so that the emperor could enter it as soon as he emerged from the building.

The bearers would eventually deliver the emperor to the Studio of Convivial Delight (*Tongyu Xuan*) in the Lake Palaces for the imperial breakfast, but only after he had visited the Palace of Earthly Tranquillity, where a dirge of Manchu shamanic music pierced the dawn light. This signalled the morning worship of Manchu gods within the imperial household. The worship of heaven was a separate matter, conducted at a special shrine called a *tangzi*, built in 1645 at a site that is today occupied by the Grand Hotel on Chang'an Boulevard.

Although the hymns invoked the gold- and silver-tongued avian deities of the Manchus, the imperial household pantheon also included the Sakyamuni Buddha, the Goddess of Mercy (*Guanyin*) and Guan Di (a Chinese martial hero by the name of Guan Yu who had been elevated to become the God of War). Twelve sacrificial celebrants and officials, including two musicians, conducted the dawn service. Also attending was Qianlong's empress Ulanara, who wore an elaborate, swaying crown studded with precious stones – pearls from the Sungari river, cat's eyes, lapis lazuli, coral and turquoise – and held in place by gold pins and filigree. Ulanara invoked the Manchu deity popularly known as Fodo-mama, the goddess of the willow frond and fertility, to protect her ancestors and progeny. Those attending the ceremony on this day could see that the empress was not in good health, although they were not to know that she only had one year to live. On conclusion of the morning worship, it was Manchu tradition that a pig be sacrificed, for which daily practice the central hall of the Palace of Earthly Tranquillity had been transformed into a vast kitchen. After the animal was slaughtered and the blood drained, it was partially cooked and the greasy unsalted 'sacrificial' meat was distributed among members of the household; partaking of this unappetising fare was a Manchu sacrament jealously fought over.

However, on this morning, when Qianlong went to the morning sacrifice, he did not participate at any length in the rituals. Instead, he spent the hour before sunrise 'communing with the ancestors'. As the Manchus became acculturated to Han Chinese practice and diet, near-raw pork came to lose its appeal. By the closing days of the Qing dynasty the practice of holding sacrifices in the Palace of Earthly Tranquillity had become the subject of jokes. A popular Chinese ditty mocked it thus: 'The windows made of paper obscure the world outside; and the old girls on the inside can't be seen for all the smoke.' The Palace of Earthly Tranquillity was only occasionally swept and unbelievably grubby and, with the exception of the months during which it served as the honeymoon abode of a newly married emperor and empress, no one lived there.

While the imperial clan adhered to their shamanist beliefs, there was room for other religions, including Buddhism and Taoism. Incense and candles were constantly being offered at as many as twenty-six shrines within the Forbidden City. Qianlong lavished particular attention on the palace's Buddhist temples; he even asserted his faith by having himself painted in the guise of a Tibetan-style sage. He reconstructed the Ming-era Pavilion of Rain and Flowers (*Yuhua Ge*) in the north-west of the palace (now the most complete Tibetan Tantric temple in China). The roof of the pavilion was cast entirely from bronze, including the Tibetan *chörten* that forms its centre and the extraordinary rearing dragons that appear to hover vigilantly above.

Beyond the exigencies of sacrificial meat and formal banquets, meals seem to have been a relatively frugal affair, although there are surprisingly few records of the culinary tastes of particular emperors. Even though there was a *Ledger of Periodic Intake* and *Ledger of the Imperial Kitchens*, these focus on a meticulous accounting of the dozens of dishes placed for display on the large dining tables, not on what the emperor or empress actually ate. As with so many aspects of imperial daily life, the details were top secret and our knowledge is thus often anecdotal. Only the observations of the eating habits of the Empress Dowager Cixi by the ladies of the Western diplomatic corps in the early twentieth century provide eyewitness accounts of what pleased the imperial palate. But even then we cannot be sure that what the

Empress Dowager liked to be seen to eat and what she liked to eat were one and the same.

The Emperor's Kitchen was located south of the Gate of Mental Cultivation (*Yangxin Men*): here the Jiajing Emperor of the Ming dynasty had heated up his lead-based elixirs and it was in this environment of blackened silver implements that Gerbillon had originally been accommodated by Kangxi until his son Yongzheng re-located the imperial kitchen there. The kitchen that served food for the emperor had one hundred timber- and coal-fired stoves, each attended by three chefs. In all, the staff of the emperor's kitchen numbered between three and four hundred. Cooked dishes were taken from the kitchens sealed in yellow silk wrappings, and they were not allowed to be opened between the kitchen and the table, to safeguard against poison. Cooks oversaw every stage of the preparation from chopping and cleaning through to the finishing touches. All food was served on silver because poisons visibly react with its surface.

The empress, dowager empress and court ladies all had their own kitchens. A system of mutual oversight was introduced in the palace kitchens. They were run by a consolidated directorship that ensured that cooks and the supply of food were segregated. The Yongzheng Emperor made the directorship a security post, reflecting the imperial clan's acute fear of poisoning.

A close examination of the *Ledger of the Imperial Kitchens* over centuries points to some trends in the imperial appetite. Before the Qianlong Emperor, rulers were fond of venison, bear, chicken, beef and lamb. There is no mention of pork, that being sacramental fare. During Qianlong's reign, swallows' nest and duck dominated the menu, although some

17. Looking out over the South Lake from Ocean Terrace to the Tower for Delighting in the Moon in the Lake Palaces. The tower is now New China Gate, the formal entrance to the Communist Party's seat of government.

old Manchu delicacies continued to be popular – deer's tails and tendons and dog meat, for example, although they were less common. The later Manchu–Han Complete Banquet (*Man-Han quanxi*, see chapter 8) assumed its definitive form during the reign of Qianlong; many accounts note that Shandong cuisine (*Lu cai*), still the basis of Beijing cooking, and humble dumplings (*jiaozi*, then called *huntun*) were palace staples.

At 5 a.m. the emperor had an early morning drink of iced and sweetened swallows' nest soup. According to the *Ledger of the Imperial Kitchens*, he finally made it to breakfast proper at 6 a.m. in the Studio of Convivial Delight. The journey to this loggia in the complex at the Lake Palaces entailed a leisurely ride in the heated palanquin. In addition to the four eunuch bearers, eight other eunuchs carried lanterns and household objects, such as a spittoon made of gold, at the front of the procession. The palanquin left the Forbidden City via the West Flourishing Gate (*Xihua Men*) and to the West Garden Gate (*Xiyuan Men*) leading into the Lake Palaces, then travelled around the southern shore of the South Lake, past many buildings and vistas until it reached the Studio of Convivial Delight which stood beside the Tower for Delighting in the Moon (*Baoyue Lou*) (converted in the early twentieth century into New China Gate, the main entrance to the Lake Palaces, see page 155). Both of these buildings had only recently been constructed to provide a new vista on to the South Lake and the island called Ocean Terrace (*Ying Tai*). In accordance with palace protocol, Qianlong ate breakfast alone, the meal of eighteen dishes from meats and sweets to dumplings and soups having been already arrayed on four large tables by the time he entered the room. Four eunuchs waited on the imperial presence, passing him the dishes and providing him with extra portions if he commented that anything was 'not bad'. The tables were heavy with the finest porcelain from the imperial kilns, as well as items made from gold, silver, agate, jade and cloisonné, most of them decorated with auspicious motifs and words of benediction such as 'ten thousand years of boundless life' (*wanshou wujiang*). The Qianlong Emperor, who was renowned for gobbling down his food, consumed his breakfast in less than fifteen minutes. The leftovers were then carefully wrapped and distributed, according to the emperor's instructions, to the palace women and princes who would receive the imperial largesse in kneeling gratitude in the courtyards of their apartments.

At 6.30 a.m. the emperor was carried back to his study in the Palace of Heavenly Purity. Although this palace had contained the sleeping quarters of the Ming rulers, the Kangxi and Qianlong emperors held large banquets there, and a sizeable reading room containing valuable antiquities had been created in its Western Heated Chamber. Maps and long scroll paintings produced by the cartographers and painters of the palace workshops were held in this reading room. Immense desks enabled Qianlong to unroll and view works such as the twelve scrolls which made up *The Qianlong Emperor's Southern Expedition*, measuring an average of 2.5 metres each in length. Whenever Qianlong was in the Forbidden City, he would spend time after breakfast in one of his studies – either in the Palace of Heavenly Purity or in the Hall of Mental Cultivation – reading through the *Veritable Records* and imperial decrees of his predecessors, but mostly studying the documentary records of the reigns of his grandfather and father. These archives were kept in the offices of the Grand

Secretariat, which delivered the material to be read by the emperor in the morning on the previous day. This ongoing review of and reference to historical precedents was part of a rigorous imperial education that had begun for Qianlong when he was only five. Once he had mastered primers at the age of eight, he had been taught by tutors from the Hanlin Academy which employed the leading scholars in the land. Although he was also trained by his Manchu uncles in the use of firearms and horseback archery, his immersion in Chinese and Confucian culture was total.

While Qianlong was having his breakfast, twenty-four of his favourite officials had been waiting outside the Gate of Heavenly Purity as they had done since before dawn for an extended morning 'tea party' (*chayan*) with the emperor. That was to take place in the Palace of Double Brilliance, located in the area of the Forbidden City where Qianlong had lived when he was still a young prince (the *Qianxi Ersuo*, mentioned in chapter 3). After Qianlong became emperor, the area was refurbished and the buildings renamed so it became a centre for family and social events. The gathering on this day was to be for the purposes of composing poems. Between 7 a.m. and 8 a.m., the emperor changed his costume and then, after resting in the Palace of Established Happiness (*Jianfu Gong*), he attended the tea party with his close officials until 10 a.m. The participants were served tea and light refreshments by the numerous attendants who performed their duties in respectful silence. In proceedings initiated by the emperor, he composed three lines of poetry on the theme of snow, thus dictating what rhymes the next participant had to use to complete the quatrain. In this case it was Fuheng, a member of the Manchu Bordered Yellow Banner (*Xianghuang Qi*), the younger brother of Qianlong's late empress Xiaoxian and his chief military adviser. Fuheng, in turn, composed three lines on a similar theme and the next participant would repeat the performance.

Qianlong was one of the most prolific poets of all time, with an oeuvre that totals nearly 50,000 verses, a daunting if not exactly brilliant output described unkindly by the famous twentieth-century scholar Qian Zhongshu as 'nauseating'. In Qianlong's defence, however, one could at least argue that he was well tutored by Shen Deqian, the leading poet of the age. Moreover, in his pursuit of his muse he enjoyed the assistance of an army of scribes, copyists and annotators, the latter able to turn careless errors into proof of arcane erudition. He certainly did devote a lot of time to writing poetry and composing couplets, something made evident on many of the buildings in the Forbidden City and in the garden palaces outside Beijing, which carry these compositions in Qianlong's stolid calligraphic hand. On this day alone he was engaged in the pursuit for nearly three hours.

Qianlong's passion for poetry did not dampen his delight in more populist forms of cultural entertainment, however, such as the theatre. He was so enthusiastic about theatre, in fact, that he had numerous theatres and stages built in the Forbidden City alone. One of these was an extraordinary indoor theatre located in his retirement palace. Called the Studio of Exhausted Diligence (*Juanqin Zhai*), a place for the emperor to recover from his administrative exertions, it contains an unusual roofed stage. The ceiling above it is a painted wisteria trellis and it is surrounded by a *trompe l'oeil* of the palace itself said to be the work of Giuseppe Castiglione.

18. A plaque in Manchu and Chinese over the entrance of the Hall for Cultivation of Character, one of the main buildings in the Qianlong Emperor's retirement palace in the Forbidden City. Many buildings and gates in the palace have plaques in both languages, while major monuments built during the multi-ethnic Qing dynasty carried inscriptions in the four official languages of the empire: Manchu, Chinese, Mongolian and Tibetan.

The most impressive theatre of Qianlong that we can see today is the Pavilion of Delightful Melodies (*Changyin Ge*), a three-storey, three-stage outdoor theatre located on the eastern side of the Hall of Peaceful Longevity (*Ningshou Gong*) in his retirement palace. Epic theatrical works with simultaneous events in heaven, earth and the underworld could be performed on these three stages, which featured elaborate staircases, machinery and amplification facilities that allowed gods and spirits to appear from the skies through 'heaven holes', or to emerge from the depths through 'earth holes' to participate in the often raucous action.

After the poetry gathering, the emperor returned to his office in the Hall of Mental Cultivation at 10 a.m. to spend the next three hours reading memorials and government documents, in both Chinese and Manchu. The laborious process of first reading such documents, many of which were sent from the provinces and covered every manner of issue from the most important to the trivial, and then responding to them often in vermilion rescripts written directly on the memorials, was for the Qing emperors the real business of government. For two hours from 1 a.m. onwards, in the same office, Qianlong received officials to discuss matters of state and approve appointments and was served his 'late meal' (*wanshan*). At 3 p.m. he had a short siesta then received the documents from the various boards of the Grand Secretariat as well as memorials from governors and local officials. At 4 p.m. he had 'late pastries' (*wanmian*) with Fuheng, with whom he discussed matters related to the army and the borderlands.

Following his official duties, at 5 p.m. the emperor repaired to the Room of the Three Rarities (*Sanxi Tang*) in the Hall of Mental Cultivation to enjoy his antiquities for two hours. His collection contained many works acquired by his predecessors as well as paintings, calligraphic works and objects an appreciation for which Qianlong had gained through his contact with the culture of the Chinese literati heartland, the Lower Yangtze Valley (*Jiangnan*). Kangxi and Yongzheng had both been fond of the southern-style gardens from this region, and Qianlong brought the passion of a builder to the expansion of his patrimony. Even though the overall ground plan of the Forbidden City had been determined in the Ming dynasty (especially during the rebuilding of the complex during the Wanli and Tianqi reigns of 1573–1627) and offered little scope for modification, both Kangxi and Qianlong designed numerous landscaped gardens to provide space for leisure and relaxation within the severe confines of the palace. Of the four gardens open to the public, the Garden of the Palace of Tranquil Longevity (*Ningshou Gong Huayuan*), also sometimes simply called the Qianlong Garden, was laid out in 1772 in the north-east precinct (the 'retirement zone') of the Forbidden City. Qianlong would make it a venue for poetry gatherings. Covering 6.4 hectares it was sub-divided into four square courts. (Only the two southern courtyards are open to the public.)

Of the gardens in the Forbidden City, this was the one most influenced by the garden culture of the south. Hills with mazes and tunnels fashioned from exotically shaped river rocks create varied vistas which break up the space and enhance its perspectives. Entering the first court, the visitor can see to the left an open-sided belvedere that sits facing a towering assemblage of rocks. Named the Pavilion to Enjoy the Pure Water Ceremony (*Xishang Ting*), it is a replica of the Orchid Pavilion (*Lan Ting*), a famous belvedere in Shaoxing,

Zhejiang province. The Orchid Pavilion was where Wang Xizhi, China's most venerated calligrapher, created his masterpiece, *Preface to the Poems Composed at the Orchid Pavilion* (*Lanting Xu*), while celebrating the ancient waterside ritual of spring purification (*xiuxi*) in the year 353. The preface is a meditation on transience and it is regarded as a classic of Chinese prose, while Wang's exquisite calligraphy, which is as the translator H. C. Chang says 'a magnificent document in the history of the Chinese sensibility', would be a model for all later writers. As Wang wrote in his preface:

> *It is idle to pretend that life and death are equal states and foolish to claim that a youth cut off in his prime has led the protracted life of a centenarian. For men of a later age will look upon our time as we look upon earlier ages – a chastening reflection.*

Qianlong visited the original pavilion in Shaoxing in 1751. Into the raised stone floor of the replicated belvedere in the Forbidden City, the emperor's masons were instructed to carve a meandering, but slightly inclined, channel. At imperial literati gatherings, cups of wine were floated down this channel. Whenever a floating cup steadied before one of the scholars he had to drink and compose a poem to match the rhymes created by the previous player, exactly in the manner described in Wang Xizhi's ancient essay.

Qianlong's pavilion not only reveals his appreciation of Lower Yangtze Valley culture, but also his material emulation of Han Chinese high culture. The Room of the Three Rarities in the westernmost alcove of his apartments in the Hall of Mental Cultivation was named after the three prizes of his collection. For he had in his possession the famous

Three Rarities of Calligraphy (*Sanxi Tie*), comprising Wang Xizhi's *Clearing After Snowfall* (*Kuaixue Shi Qing Tie*), his son Wang Xianzhi's *Mid-Autumn Letter* (*Zhongqiu Tie*) and Wang Xun's *Letter to Boyuan* (*Boyuan Tie*), all dating from the fourth century and regarded as three of the greatest masterpieces of calligraphic art.

The Three Rarities are said to have been acquired for Qianlong's grandfather Kangxi by his tutor Gao Shiqi. It seems that Qianlong, unlike Kangxi and Gao, was unaware that Wang Xianzhi's *Mid-Autumn Letter* and Wang Xun's *Letter to Boyuan* were in fact copies most probably made during either the Tang or the Song dynasties. Whenever the Qianlong Emperor discovered that he had acquired a forgery, he liked to play a little joke on his highly educated officials, inviting them to sign the work and add their prefatory comments to the margins as if it were the genuine article. So Qianlong clearly had a sense of humour, if not always a discerning eye. For he himself never knew that the works that formed the centrepiece of his own connoisseurship were forgeries. He might not have been so amused had he found out.

At 7 p.m. he relaxed for an hour and then, at 8 p.m., he retired to the Eastern Heated Chamber (*Dong Nuange*) of the Hall of Mental Cultivation to sleep. So came to an end the emperor's working day. Qianlong's reign was rich in incident that reflected a confident ruler dealing with the vicissitudes of an expanding empire, the constant movement of officials and a dexterous handling of Manchu relations with the Han Chinese élite. There were many occasions during his long career when the rituals of state filled his hours, or delicate negotiations were reflected in the elaborate paperwork that crossed his desk. But this day, 28 January 1765, although interspersed with cultural pursuits, was neither tinged with frivolity nor laden with pomp and ceremony. It was one seemingly not even animated by intrigue.

5

....

THE DOWAGER

North of the Hall of Mental Cultivation, the main residence of Qing emperors into the early twentieth century, runs a long avenue from which broad lanes lead into the Western Six Palaces, an extensive complex of courtyards and buildings which once housed part of the imperial seraglio. One of these is the Palace of Accumulated Elegance (*Chuxiu Gong*). Lavishly refurbished in 1884 on the occasion of the fiftieth birthday of the Empress Dowager Cixi and her ostensible retirement in favour of her nephew and adopted son, the Guangxu Emperor, this palace witnessed some of the major events of the closing years of the dynasty.

From the Ming dynasty onwards, imperial custom decreed that the emperor's mother (or imperial women of her generation) would quit the Western Six Palaces once their child ascended the throne. Empresses dowager relocated their personal apartments to one of the spacious residences arranged along the Forbidden City's western perimeter. These included the Palace of Benevolent Tranquillity and its extensive gardens, the Palace of Longevity and Health and the Palace of Peaceful Longevity. (Currently closed to the public, these buildings house offices of the Palace Museum.)

The many dwellings here, built in the style of typical courtyard houses of north China, were home to the numerous wives and companions of deceased emperors, as well as the harem of the present ruler. Qing imperial consorts were divided into eight ranks: there was one Empress (*huanghou*); one Imperial Noble Consort (*huang guifei*); two Noble Consorts (*guifei*); four Consorts (*fei*); six Imperial Concubines (*pin*); and no fixed number of Honoured Ladies (*guiren*), The Ever-Present (*changzai*) and Those Who Comply (*daying*). This system of imperial rankings determined the women's status and every aspect of their lives: the location, size and decoration of their apartments; their costume, jewellery and headdress; their ceremonial duties; the quality of their food and tea; as well as the number of eunuchs and female servants at their beck and call.

Born into the noble Manchu Yehonala clan in 1835, the future Empress Dowager Cixi had entered the Forbidden City at the age of sixteen during the triennial selection of palace girls from among the Manchu families favoured by the court. She had been given the simple name of Lan, meaning Orchid; her name and place of residence changed with every elevation in her rank. An attractive and talented girl, she soon enjoyed the royal favour, to become one of the eighteen women of various rank in the seraglio of the Xianfeng Emperor ('prosperity for all', r. 1851–61). As a result, she moved into the Palace of Terrestrial Assistance and, in 1854, she was promoted to the rank of Imperial Concubine and henceforth titled Yi, the Virtuous. When, in 1856, she gave birth to the emperor's only son and heir, she was elevated to Consort and was known as the Virtuous Consort (*Yi Fei*). Thereafter she was given the title and rank of Virtuous Noble Consort (*Yi Guifei*), only two levels below the empress herself.

As mother of the new ruler the Virtuous Noble Consort was elevated to the rank of Empress Dowager (*huang taihou*) following the death of the Xianfeng Emperor, and bestowed with the name Cixi ('benevolent and auspicious'). She was now on near parity with the Xianfeng Emperor's empress proper, who henceforth was known as the Empress Dowager Ci'an ('benevolent and tranquil'). After a palace coup orchestrated in complicity with the dead emperor's brother Prince Gong ('the respectful', 1833–98), the two dowagers ruled over the empire as co-regents while Cixi's son, the Tongzhi Emperor ('joint rule', r. 1862–74), was too young to exercise power in his own right. A remarkable attempt to modernise the country was launched by Prince Gong and his allies, both Manchu and Han Chinese, during that period, which became known as the 'Tongzhi Restoration' (*Tongzhi zhongxing*). However, the prince eventually fell out with the emperor and Cixi, and the widely supported reforms were curtailed.

At the beginning of their regency the empresses dowager continued to live in the Western Six Palaces, which afforded ready access to the emperor's residence in the Hall of Mental Cultivation. For convenience they also had apartments within the emperor's quarters so that they could attend to matters of state during the daily imperial audience. The Tongzhi Emperor died at the age of eighteen, plagued, it is said, by illness brought on by carnal excess (he had already gathered five women in his harem). Despite his indulgence, however, he had failed to produce an heir. His cousin, Cixi's nephew, was therefore installed on the throne as the Guangxu Emperor, his reign title meaning 'glorious succession', disguising the plangent state of the imperial clan. This prompted Cixi to move to her new quarters at the Palace of Accumulated Elegance; due to her seniority her co-regent Ci'an occupied more spacious apartments in the Eastern Six Palaces.

The under-age emperors – first Tongzhi and then Guangxu – were guided by the two matriarchs who ruled, literally, 'from behind the screen' (*chui lian ting zheng*): sitting on thrones concealed by a screen behind the emperor's throne during audiences in the Hall of Mental Cultivation. The short lives and reigns of the last rulers of the Qing were regarded as being of ominous portent, and indeed the early demise of Sons of Heaven had bedevilled imperial politics in China for over 2000 years. There have been a total of 557 emperors since the First Emperor of the Qin dynasty, including the rulers of minor states which occupied the territory of what is modern China; only one of them lived beyond the age of eighty (Qianlong, who lived to eighty-eight). Only four survived into their seventies, eighteen into their sixties and less than one in ten made it to their fifties. More than half of China's emperors only attained the age of thirty. On average, an emperor could expect to rule for less than four years. The most long-lived emperors were those of the Qing, their average lifespan being fifty-one years. The rulers with the shortest life expectancy were the child-emperors of the Eastern Han dynasty (25–220 CE). On average, they did not survive into their thirties; the rulers of the precursors of the Qing dynasty, the Ming, were also short-lived, over two-thirds of them dying before their fortieth year.

The early death of her own son, the premature passing of her co-regent Ci'an in 1881 (by poison if the rumours are to be believed) and the sidelining of the Guangxu Emperor in an exercise of extraordinary political wile allowed the Empress Dowager Cixi to rule China, either from 'behind the screen' or in her own right through 'political tutelage' (*xun zheng*), until her own demise in 1908 at the age of seventy-three.

慈禧垂帘听政展

19. 'An Exhibition of Cixi's Rule from Behind the Screen', a sign in the alley at the entrance to the Palace of Accumulated Elegance. The image of the Empress Dowager is based on a painting by the American artist Katherine A. Carl who was commissioned to paint Cixi's portrait at her garden residences at the Sea Palaces and the Summer Palace. This picture is a copy of the portrait that was finally displayed on a specially built mount at the Palace of Fine Arts at the St Louis World Exposition in 1904.

Today, the Western Six Palaces are still unrestored. Their courtyards are forlorn, their flagstones uneven; the ancient cypresses are writhen and decrepit; the meticulous Suzhou-style paintings decorating the eves of the palace buildings have lost their lustre and are peeling, and the vermilion columns are dull and flaking. The once brilliant golden glazed roof tiles are friable, clumps of grass growing in their cracks, and the glass windows of the studios, rooms and halls are darkened by the countless fingerprints of tourists straining to gain a glimpse of the erstwhile private world of the most powerful – and reviled – woman in Chinese history. The royal apartments form part of a display called 'Cixi's Rule from Behind the Screen', a dusty and neglected exhibition that outlines her supposedly ruthless rise to power and her corrupt and autocratic rule over the tottering Qing empire. The evidence of her extravagant lifestyle – the gold and silver chopsticks, spoons and bowls, the elaborate hair ornaments and bejewelled geegaws – might have affronted the impoverished peasantry in the Maoist past. Now, if anything, they appear modest, tasteful and less than opulent to the new generation of visitors, many of whom themselves enjoy a sumptuous standard of living – the boom-era yuppies and latter-day princelings who live in the gated communities dotted around Beijing and its environs, in palatial residences rejoicing in such names as 'Imperial Villa', 'Royal Retreat' or 'Detached Palace'.

Just as the economic revival of China helps put dynastic excess into perspective, so too have distance and time cast new light on the Empress Dowager, arguably the last great incumbent of the Forbidden City. Gradually, the stories told by both Chinese and Western journalists and scholars of the evil and scheming shrew at the centre of China's late-imperial decline are being undermined by more balanced historical opinion and nuanced evaluation. Indeed, it is now more widely appreciated that the empresses dowager acted entirely within accepted dynastic practice when they assumed power with Prince Gong in 1861 – the women in the Manchu court had been regularly, and effectively, involved in everyday politics. However, this tradition differed from those of the Han Chinese, and it was this which gave rise to some of the more histrionic and misogynistic claims of female abuse of power. The radical Han Chinese opponents of the Empress Dowager Cixi, together with the tireless efforts of key Western journalists who despised the ruling house, created a successful international propaganda campaign against the late Qing rulers in general, and Cixi in particular. Subsequently, Han Chinese patriots and Marxist historians of the Republican era portrayed the rule of the Manchu invaders and the vanished Qing dynasty in a relentlessly negative light. And so, despite recent scholarly reappraisal, these collective prejudices still powerfully colour the popular view of the Empress Dowager and Qing rule.

In her later years, Cixi moved to the Palace of Tranquil Longevity (*Ningshou Gong*), the luxurious apartments along the eastern side of the Forbidden City that the Qianlong Emperor had built for his retirement over a hundred years earlier. This broad corridor of palaces occupies a self-contained area from the east of the Archery Pavilion to the northernmost wall of the Forbidden City. Gaining access from the Gate for the Bestowal of Rewards (*Xiqing Men*) the visitor enters a courtyard, on the south side of which is a brilliantly coloured glaze-tiled Nine Dragon Screen Wall, similar to but perhaps even finer than another such wall on the northern shore of North Lake Park (*Bei Hai*) in the Lake Palaces. This formal entrance to Qianlong's palace opens into a large courtyard and grand audience chambers and buildings dedicated to the secret Manchu shamanistic religious ceremonies. As with the imperial apartments on the western side of the Forbidden City, the private quarters of Qianlong's retirement palace are situated to the north of these more public, ceremonial structures.

It was in the Palace of Tranquil Longevity that the Empress Dowager was living when the dramatic events of the summer of 1900 known as the Boxer Rebellion took place. The rebel 'Boxers', who blamed China's ills on foreigners and their 'pig religion' (Christianity), recruited an army from among the impoverished and disaffected people of north China in order to expel the foreigners from the country. On the advice of some of her more conservative courtiers, the Empress Dowager lent the Boxers her support. Joining with imperial troops in Beijing, the Boxers claimed that their esoteric religious practices had made them invincible and proceeded to lay siege to the foreign Legation Quarter. However, the leading Western powers and Japan sent a united expedition to invade China and relieve the siege of Beijing, quickly overwhelming the Boxers and the Qing army, thereby prompting the Empress Dowager and her court to undertake a hasty 'imperial hunting trip to the western provinces' (*xi shou*). The Eight-Power Allied Expeditionary Force triumphantly entered the abandoned Forbidden City in August 1900 and freely and shamelessly plundered its treasures.

The events of that summer in 1900 would play a role once more in the first years of the revolutionary order established under the People's Republic of China in 1949. Ever mindful

20. The Legation Quarter located on the right on the former site of the administrative boards of the Qing empire. On the left China Gate leads into the Corridor of a Thousand Paces towards the Gate of Heavenly Peace.

of the lingering influence of the past, the Communist Party Chairman Mao Zedong launched the first of many cultural purges with an attack on the 1948 Hong Kong film *The Secret History of the Qing Court*, which revolved around the rebellion and the inner workings of the palace. Featuring popular stars, the film, which brought up the issue of reform versus revolution that had tested Chinese thinkers and political figures throughout the twentieth century, enjoyed great popularity throughout China. But Mao saw in it a dangerously reactionary message about the late-Qing government, one that favoured political reform as opposed to 'progressive' violent uprisings like the Boxer Rebellion. This ideological clash had played out within the imperial Qing court in 1898 when the reform-minded Guangxu Emperor supported proposals for political, economic and bureaucratic change. Guangxu had been encouraged in this by his favourite concubine, the Pearl Consort (*Zhen Fei*, or Lady Tatara), played in the film by the celebrated singer Zhou Xuan. However, the emperor and his supporters had been outmanoeuvred by the Empress Dowager and the military man Yuan Shikai (see chapter 7). The reforms were overturned. Despite this, the leader of the reformist scholar officials, Kang Youwei, had, with the help of the Pearl Consort, managed to escape the Empress Dowager's murderous wrath. None the less, the re-emergence of the political conservatives in the court contributed directly to the disastrous mishandling of the Boxer Rebellion. In the film, just before the court's flight from the capital, the Empress Dowager vengefully orders the Pearl Consort be cast down a well. The emperor learns of this betrayal as they quit the capital.

In a small courtyard next to the Pavilion of Great Felicity (*Jingqi Ge*) north of the Empress Dowager's personal apartments – the Hall for the Cultivation of Character (*Yangxing Dian*), the Studio for Delightful Old Age (*Leshou Tang*) and the Pavilion for Nourishing Harmony (*Yihe Xuan*) (which today house displays of precious objects and huge carved blocks of precious milky-green jade from Hetian in Xinjiang) – there is a well covered with a large stone. This place is said to be where the Pearl Consort drowned in mysterious circumstances – possibly murdered – as the court readied to flee. (A small room nearby has been converted into a shrine dedicated to her memory.)

Historians disagree about how the Pearl Consort actually met her end. But there is no doubt as to the odium surrounding the event, or the extent to which it besmirched the already tarnished reputation of the Empress Dowager. Shortly after the demise of the dynasty, the first accounts appeared claiming that Cixi had ordered her murder. A popular version of the story holds that the insubordinate Pearl Consort had the gall to urge the emperor to remain in Beijing in order to negotiate with the advancing foreign armies. In the most colourful of the stories, the enraged Empress Dowager shouts, 'Throw this wretched minion down the well!' – whereupon the hapless young woman is flung to her death. A recent revisionist account of events by Yehonala Genzheng, the great-grandson of the Empress Dowager's younger brother Yehonala Guixiang, argues that the older woman was actually under the spell of the young consort. He claims that the Pearl Consort's acuity and independence of personality reminded Cixi of herself at that age. They were in fact quite friendly, even if Cixi did not approve of the Pearl Consort using a eunuch to smuggle a camera into the palace for her amusement, or of her dressing up in men's attire, going so far as to don some of the emperor's clothes during her photographic gambols. The Empress Dowager felt that such goings on were a flagrant breach of propriety and, furthermore, at the time she was deeply suspicious of the devilry behind photography. According to Yehonala Genzheng's account, the Pearl Consort was outraged that the emperor was being forced to flee in such ignominious circumstances. She declared that she would rather die than endure the shame, to which the Empress Dowager retorted in the heat of the moment that if the Pearl Consort wished to kill herself she should do so, whereupon the young woman impetuously threw herself down the well.

Whatever the truth may be, the flight of the court in mid-August 1900 and the extraordinary resilience of the Empress Dowager would be the source of fascination and even fantasy for a number of influential writers. The French novelist and adventurer Victor Segalen's 1922 novel *René Leys* describes an imaginary and sensual infiltration of the court. Segalen spent five years in China from 1909 and wrote a number of books about the country. *René Leys* is an extraordinary work that revels in the utter otherness of China, the mysteries of the palace and its occupants and the quest to penetrate the inner sanctum. In creating the main character of the novel, René Leys, Segalen was allegedly inspired by a young French China *savant*, Maurice Roy, a man who fantasised that he had once saved the life of the Guangxu Emperor. In a preface to a 2003 English reprint of the book, the cultural commentator Ian Buruma describes Segalen's exoticism as 'charged erotic frustration. You want to penetrate the other, but can never succeed, for otherwise the attraction, and thus the charge, would vanish.'

It is an observation that reflects, too, the abiding lure of the Forbidden City for other writers. The name René Leys would find an echo in the penname 'Simon Leys' used by Pierre Ryckmans, the art historian who wrote the most incisive and pitilessly satirical accounts of Mao-era politics in the 1970s. (His books include *The Chairman's New Clothes* published in 1971, and *Chinese Shadows* which appeared in 1976). It was a time when writers and academics in China had been silenced and so many overseas chose discretion or the path of the fellow traveller.

Far more psychologically complex and more influential than Maurice Roy because of his long years in Beijing and canny self-promotion, was the displaced Cornish aristocrat Edmund Trelawny Backhouse. The origin of much of the mischief related to Cixi in the English language is to be found in the 1905 bestseller *China under the Empress Dowager*, a confection created by this salacious fantasist and the journalist and businessman J. O. P. Bland. This work, in which Cixi appears as a malevolent viper of a woman, was to be regarded as impeccably authoritative for decades. Both authors had at various times been colleagues or assistants and informants for George E. Morrison, the influential Australian-born correspondent for *The Times* who was himself an ardent critic of the Empress Dowager during the crucial last years of the Qing dynasty.

China under the Empress Dowager promised startling revelations about the secret manipulations of the court during the Boxer Rebellion. It also claimed to reveal hitherto unknown details about the goings on at the heart of the enigmatic Chinese empire. Included in it was a translation of *The Diary of His Excellence Jingshan*, supposedly an insider's record of events surrounding the Boxer Rebellion. In reality, the diary was an elaborate confabulation, the product of the fecund imagination of Edmund Backhouse, whose mastery of Chinese was such that even his co-author did not question the work's veracity. After the Boxer Rebellion the world was eager for the story of a depraved and barbaric Chinese court and its capricious female ruler and *China under the Empress Dowager* was greeted with what the historian Lo Hui-min called a 'tidal wave of eulogies':

> *The popular press led the way in ensuring the book's success: news-papers and journals in which China had hitherto found no place now rushed into print to hail its appearance. Critics everywhere, not to be outshone by their peers, showered it with extravagant expressions of appreciation, as if no praise were high enough. In a seemingly unending crescendo, readers from Glasgow to Dunedin, from Toronto to Johannesburg, were told that this was 'an indispensable guide through the bewildering maze of Chinese politics'; that it was 'the most informing book on Chinese affairs that has appeared within a decade'; that it 'throws more light on the internal history of Peking than all the books written about China during the last quarter of a century'; that it was 'without question one of the most important contributions to contempo-rary historical literature which has been made in our time ...'*

It would be decades before the mendacity of much of the book was revealed, and the forgery of the diary was only uncovered in 1936 (and proved in 1940). In his important early 1990s revisionist account of the Empress Dowager, *Dragon Lady*, the writer Sterling Seagrave aptly concludes that the 'bloodthirsty caricature of Cixi was a clever blend of Western fantasy and Chinese pornography'.

For Backhouse, however, when it came to penetrating the Forbidden City, *China under the Empress Dowager* was little more than foreplay. In his declining years he wrote his memoirs, perhaps with the *succès d'estime* of Segalen's *René Leys* still in mind. In *Décadence Manchoue*, a still-unpublished account of his early years in Beijing, Backhouse reveals a connoisseur's delectation for the inner workings and carnal pleasures of the imperial boudoir; moreover, he does so in a manner unparalleled in the colonial-era writings of China obsessives, bringing to the task not only a highly developed erotic imagination but an extraordinary breadth of reading in the literature of China and of the Greek, Latin and French classics. Backhouse's Forbidden City is both the repository of his huge learning and the projection of his own unfulfilled sexual fantasies, dating back to an adolescence spent in another, equally ancient 'closed world', the medieval cloisters of Winchester College.

Writing from his hospital bed in Japanese-occupied Beiping (as the city of Beijing was once more known from 1928 to 1949), Backhouse offers a 'recollection' of his first sexual dalliance with the long-dead Empress Dowager. Although often referred to, Backhouse's account is rarely if ever directly quoted. Given the prudish sensibilities of the past, perhaps this is understandable.

[The chief eunuch] Li accompanied me to the phoenix couch, and the Empress exclaimed: 'My bed is cold: come and soothe my loneliness.' Li said: 'Kneel down on the cushion and let the Old Buddha caress your behind and before.' 'Nonsense,' said the Empress, 'how in the world can he do what he wants to do in a kneeling posture! Let him disclose his bounteous nudity; for I wish to feast my eyes on his personal charms' …

'You must forget that I am empress: regard me as Yang Guifei and yourself as Tang Minghuang, that poetic Son of Heaven.' 'How could I dare, Old Buddha? To me Your Majesty is Aval-okitesvara, the Goddess of Mercy, ever young, ever fair; what the Catholics call "Stella Maris", the star of hope which emergeth from the sea and symbolizeth peace and harmony, even as the Blessed Virgin of their Faith' …

'Flatterer! Now exhibit to me your genitals, for I know I shall love them.' I had by this time an enormous orgasm and the Old Buddha fondled my verge and glans penis, kissing many times the urethral orifice or 'meatus' (mayan) which was saturated in the exotic perfume. Then she played with my voluminous scrotum, and I thought of Juvenal's decidedly uncomplimentary fourth satire on women, 'Sic volo sic jubeo,' where the slave's genitals are discussed … Next the Empress took my penis into her mouth and continued titillation with her tongue. God was very good, and I had no ejaculation, as the potency of the drug retarded the flow of sperm. She bade me contemplate her august Person and I admired the abundant wealth of pubic hair, while at her command I took in my hands her abnormally large clitoris, pressed toward it my lips and performed a low but steady friction which increased its size. She graciously unveiled the mysteries of her swelling vulva, even as that of Messalina, and I marvelled at the perennial youth which its abundance seemed to indicate …

As I expected she next told me to kneel over the couch in full glare of the garish light and the reflection of the mirrors which pre-sented the counterfeit resemblance of my buttocks which she gra-ciously likened to a peach; she minutely inspected the fundament until she bade me open up with my two forefingers and caressed it with her long-nailed index, inserting it (to my discomfort) inside the anus. Then she drew closer and brought her erect clitoris into *juxtaposition of my 'trou fignon' which she poetically compared to a rose-bud. She worked the member (which Marie Antoinette so loved in the princesse de Lamballe) backward and forward inside my anus; until, after perhaps five minutes or more, the gratifying titillation caused her to exclaim: 'Shufu', 'Hao shou', Agreeable, pleasing sensation. I cannot explain why, but a definite discharge of a sticky fluid wetted me in and around the anal cavity.*

It was a fantasy that brings to mind the comment by a Frenchman that Cixi was 'the only man in China', a role reversal of the trope of prostrate nineteenth-century China being penetrated by the Western powers. It also pre-dates by over half a century the theme of the hit 1993 Chinese television series *A Beijing Man in New York* in which the Chinese protagonist Wang Qiming hires an American prostitute and, as he penetrates her, showers her with greenbacks demanding she cry out 'I love you, I love you'.

In post-Mao China, the image of the Eastern and Western Palaces lived on in a famous gay beat next to the Gate of Heavenly Peace. In the old Imperial City wall on either side of the raised spectator platforms flanking the gate were built two public toilets called, in the local argot, 'the Eastern and Western Palaces' (*Dong Gong* and *Xi Gong*) respectively, the names once used for the Empresses Dowager Ci'an (who lived in the Eastern Palaces) and Cixi (who lived in the Western Palaces). Appropriately enough, the semi-independent film-maker Zhang Yuan named the first documentary about gay subculture in the Chinese capital *East Palace West Palace*.

The Empress Dowager emerged again as a pivotal cultural figure as Mao's own rule waned in the 1970s – the later years of Mao's life themselves being described by many writers, both in China and overseas, as resembling those of a senescent emperor (see chapter 7 below). His wife, Jiang Qing, who played a major role in creating a revolutionary culture from the 1960s, gave a self-indulgent interview to the American academic Roxanne Witke for her book entitled in English *Comrade Chiang Ch'ing* (1977), but far more famous in its Chinese translation published in Hong Kong under the title *Empress of the Red Capital* (*Hongdu nühuang*). After she fell from power, Jiang Qing was disparaged as a woman with imperial pretensions. Her critics attacked her for being a latter-day Empress Lü of the Han (second century) or Empress Wu (of the Tang) or Empress Dowager Cixi, scheming to grab power following her husband's demise. Cixi was known for enjoying her gardens and fruit trees; ironically, on the night of her arrest on 6 October 1976, Jiang Qing had gone to pluck fruit on Prospect Hill, the artificial mountain behind the palace which, on her orders, had been closed to the public for some years for her private use.

Before that, however, as Jiang Qing was rising to cultural prominence in the early 1960s, a popular film about the Empress Dowager and the Boxer siege of Beijing was enjoying an enthusiastic international release. Directed by Nicholas Ray, famed for his 1955 film *Rebel Without a Cause*, *55 Days at Peking* reveals the rebels in a very different light from the tale told in revolutionary China, where the Boxers are still regarded as a progressive social movement. The publicity tagline for this 1963 movie was: 'A handful of men and women hold out against the frenzied hordes of bloodthirsty fanatics!' In it the Australian dancer Robert 'Sir Bobby' Helpmann, decked out in full court attire, plays a devious, Fu Manchu-like evil minister. Based on the historical Prince Duan, who

21. 'Mother of God, Empress of China'. The Chinese Jesuit artist Siméon Lieou used another painting by Katherine A. Carl of Cixi, who was called the 'holy mother' of the Qing dynasty, as a model for this popular image. In this modern interpretation of that picture, Mary is seated on a throne in Manchu imperial costume with a baby 'emperor Jesus' on her knee. Our Lady of Donglu became famous after the congregation of Donglu in Hebei province miraculously escaped a Boxer onslaught. Their church became a popular pilgrimage site for Chinese Catholics.

supported the xenophobic Boxers, Helpmann's character waves his long fingers with their talon-like nails protected by metal sheaths studded with precious stones while ordering a display of Boxer kung-fu at the British Legation. Subsequently, he is seen directing a group of Boxers who ambush and kill the German minister, Baron Clemens Freiherr von Ketteler, in one of the key events leading up to the siege of the Legation Quarter.

At court the prince pits himself against General Ronglu (played by Leo Genn). He is supported by the Empress Dowager, who utters obscure phrases in shrill tones and attempts to save her dynasty by declaring war on the imperial powers. The film set of the Forbidden City, built on the outskirts of Madrid and peopled by overseas Chinese kitchen hands, shows the palace separated from the Legation Quarter by only a single gate, rather than as it is in reality, a kilometre distant with many intervening walls, alleys and roads. Inside the massive fake palace is a crude replica of the majestic Hall of Bountiful Harvests (*Qinian Dian*) at the Altar of Heaven in the south of Beijing (actually over three kilometres beyond the southernmost point of the Forbidden City). Here, in a cavernous, incense-filled circular throne room-*cum*-lair, the Empress Dowager rules with absolute power. Gates open and soldiers carry in a palanquin in which Ronglu is seated, as the film's narrator intones, 'Here in untouchable isolation lives the Dowager Empress, last of the Manchus. Protected by an army of eunuchs, she holds court and consults with her ministers, mandarins and generals.' Prince Duan is outraged to see an execution he ordered being aborted by Ronglu. He goes to complain to the monarch. She is in her royal garden (bizarrely situated next to the execution ground), absorbed in discussion with her prognosticators. They are contemplating the auguries to determine whether her beloved nightingale will recover from an illness. There is no emperor, no council of ministers, merely Her Transcendence, a figure who, when confronted with the conflicting opinions of her advisers, utters such deathless lines as, 'The voice of the nightingale is still; I hear only the sound of crows.' She overrules Ronglu and orders that the execution of the innocent man proceed as he has 'disturbed the tranquillity of the morning'.

The Empress Dowager was played by Flora Robson, an actor well known for performances as a screen monarch, having previously appeared as the Russian Empress Elisabeth in *The Rise of Catherine the Great* (1934) and Queen Elizabeth I in Alexander Korda's *Fire Over England* (1937). Her 1937 portrayal of Livia, the scheming wife of the Roman emperor Augustus, in Josef von Sternberg's unfinished *I, Claudius* daresay helped qualify her to depict an imperious woman who ruled from behind the throne. The soft-spoken British diplomat played by David Niven tells her that 'China's great-est virtue is her patience'. She responds testily, 'China is a prostrate cow. The powers are no longer content to milk her, now they are butchering her for her meat.' Later she asks her advisers, 'Who is there to make muddy water clear?'

Eventually, the Allied Expeditionary Force relieves the Legations manfully protected by Niven and a swashbuck-ling cowboy-like American (Charlton Heston) who enjoys a romantic liaison with the sultry Russian baroness Natalie Ivanoff (Ava Gardner). In the final scene, before abandon-ing the Forbidden City, the Empress Dowager wanders alone into her now empty throne room dressed in peasant garb. Distraught, she quotes the ancient philosopher Xunzi: 'Water can support a ship; and water can capsize it', to which she adds, 'The dynasty is finished.' *55 Days at Peking*, screened widely in 1963, was unintentionally to prime international audiences for the Boxer-like barbarity that was just about to engulf China in the Cultural Revolution.

As China opened its doors to the world from the late 1970s, the Qing era and its heritage again came to play a part in the nation's cultural life, even though it would be many years before more even-handed views of the last dynastic inhabitants of the Forbidden City would come to the fore. One of the first major cinematic co-productions with a non-mainland film-maker, the renowned Taiwan-based director Li Han-hsiang, led to two popular films on Qing politics and the Empress Dowager. Li's 1983 *Ruling behind the Screen* recounted the Empress Dowager's rise to fame while using the Forbidden City and the Imperial Mountain Lodge at Chengde as a backdrop to the drama. Indulging in the patriotic and highly charged ideological language of the day, the film depicts how Cixi inveigled herself into power to extend her autocratic rule over China for forty-seven years. The film also made the claim that she and her co-regent Ci'an 'were in cahoots with the Western imperialists, repressed uprisings of the people and allowed China to decline so that it became a semi-feudal, semi-colonial society. Although the people would live in dire straits, the Qing empire had started on its course to ultimate oblivion.' Such hyperbole suited the politics of China in the 1980s. Two decades were to pass before the first positive appraisal of the Empress Dowager appeared in the mass media: the popular 2003 television period drama *Towards the Republic* (*Zouxiang Gonghe*), in which Cixi is portrayed as a capable, albeit conservative, ruler.

If the Communist Party-controlled mass media is now allowed more ideological leeway in its depictions of Cixi's rule, internationally the habit of tarring her and Communist-era politics with the same obscurantist and imperial brush dies hard. The bestselling 2005 biography *Mao: The Untold Story* by Jung Chang and Jon Halliday has successfully exploited the old image of Chinese obliquity developed so venomously by journalists and writers like Morrison, Bland and Backhouse in creating its relentlessly dark portrait of Mao as tyrant. The authors speak of Mao's comrades as a 'court' and the Chinese people as his 'subjects'. The mayor of Shanghai, Ke Qingshi, is 'a favourite retainer'; People's Liberation Army Unit 8341, charged with the security of the Lake Palaces, is dubbed 'the Praetorian Guard', and its commander Wang Dongxing as the Chairman's 'trusted chamberlain'. In this landscape of caricature Premier Zhou Enlai can only be the Chairman's 'slave'. Even when Mao employs the pronoun of *faux* party fraternity, 'we', the authors claim that he was using the 'royal we'. To further emphasise Mao's inhumanity, the writers observe that his 'girlfriends were not treated like royal mistresses and showered with gifts and favours. Mao used them, as he did his wife. They provided him with sex, and served him as maids and nurses.' The admix of courtly Victoriana, Claudio-Julian terminology and China's own parlance of palace intrigue leaves the befuddled reader with a metaphorical schema that situates Mao firmly at some quaint, incomprehensible oriental remove and reduces a complex history to one of personal fiat and imperial hauteur. It is a place not that far from the world depicted by Bland and Backhouse a century earlier in *China under the Empress Dowager*.

6

....

WITHIN AND WITHOUT
THE PALACE

The Guangxu Emperor and Cixi died within a day of each other, in November 1908. Cixi had arranged that her great-nephew, a three-year-old boy by the name of Puyi, would next take the throne as the Xuantong Emperor. Despite desperate last-minute attempts to reform the government, an uprising in the south of China in October 1911 led to an anti-Manchu rebellion that quickly spread throughout the country. The regent, the Empress Dowager Longyu ('boundless plenty', empress of the Guangxu Emperor and niece of Cixi), had no choice but to negotiate with the military and reach an agreement that allowed the peaceful abdication of the emperor and the safety of the royal house in the new Republic of China.

The revolutionary leaders would vie among themselves for control over the restive new nation. Their number included hopeful democrats as well as former allies of the imperial house. The decade that followed the establishment of the Republic would see their rivalries bring the massive territory of the Qing empire close to collapse. The government of the new Republic which now replaced the ancient system of dynastic rule had come into power as a result of revolutionary uprisings. Many of its supporters were radicals who had engaged in agitation, sabotage, assassination and covert operations against the Beijing government for years. The Han Chinese would rule once more, now that the hated Manchu imperial house had been dethroned. Their military arm, the bannermen (*qiren*) soldiers who had occupied cities throughout China from the 1640s, was cashiered – and many Manchus were slaughtered in race riots. While the transition was swift, the nascent Republic of China was being constantly undermined by vacillating politicians and contending warlords. It was also immediately faced with a dilemma, one that was centred on the Forbidden City itself.

The terms of the abdication allowed what was to be known as the 'little court' (*xiao chaoting*) of the Xuantong Emperor to remain in the Inner Court of the Forbidden City. The emperor's retinue continued as before, bound to impuissant routines and rituals. Initially, the Republican rulers tolerated their presence in the defunct centre of power over which they often had little effective control. But they also had to decide what the aspiring modern nation of China should do with a palace that was a relic of a bygone age, but whose charisma still suffused the attitudes of many of their fellow citizens. While the reduced court would continue its existence 'within' the Forbidden City, it was a place 'without' any practical power. The new rulers decided that the ancient imperial enclave should be nationalised and become, literally, a museum of the past.

In the dying years of the Qing dynasty, as part of a belated attempt at modernising reform, the imperial government had established a zoological garden (opened in July 1907), a public library and a university in Beijing. But all proposals to the throne to create a public museum to showcase the imperial collections of art, books and antiquities, as well as the studios, ateliers, academies, workshops and laboratories of the Ming and Qing emperors were to fall on deaf ears. In 1905, the reformer and entrepreneur Zhang Jian urged the court to emulate Japan's Meiji Emperor and found what he called a 'royal household museum' or 'exposition' to display objects from the royal collection. But his appeal went unheeded. That same year, however, he built the country's first modern museum for the display of both cultural artefacts and modern technology, in Nantong, Jiangsu province.

Another early proponent of the creation of a state-sponsored museum was Jin Liang, director of the extensive royal palace in the original Manchu dynastic centre of Shengjing (also known as Mukden; present-day Shenyang), the 'secondary capital' (*peidu*) of the Qing empire. In 1910, he fruitlessly proposed that a gallery be set aside to display items from the collection there to the public. After the abdication of the Qing monarch, he remained in the service of the dethroned emperor, Puyi, and formally suggested on three occasions that his master display his collections.

Many of the world's museums have developed from traditions centred on eclectic 'cabinets of curiosities', or *Wunderkammern*, which appeared in the late Renaissance when there was no formal delineation between the sciences, art and the appreciation of natural wonders. They combined 'natural' and 'artificial' curiosities in private displays and mini-museums. The collections we see today in the Palace Museum in Beijing (as well as its 'sister institution' in Taiwan) by contrast almost all fall within the category of antiquities, be they bronzes, paintings, calligraphy, clocks or costumes. However, numerous Ming and Qing objects were of course not antiquities when they initially became the property of the imperial clan in the Forbidden City; many were items of tribute presented to the throne, representing the best products of the realm and beyond. Also in the palace collection are decorative arts objects that were produced in workshops within the grounds of the Forbidden City, in the garden palaces outside Beijing, or under the control of the Imperial Household Department in other parts of China. In other words, many of the 'antiquities' in the Palace Museum's collection were originally part of an exposition of contemporary manufactures.

Almost immediately following the 12 February 1912 edict of Empress Dowager Longyu announcing that she and the six-year-old emperor would abdicate, tentative steps were taken towards the creation of a national museum in the Forbidden City. Three days after the abdication, the provisional president of the new Republic of China, Sun Yat-sen, led a government delegation to pay their respects at the tomb of the founder of the Ming dynasty, the Hongwu Emperor ('abundantly martial', r. 1368–98), in Nanjing. Sun informed his august spirit that the Manchu invaders had been overthrown and that the Han Chinese were ruling a united China once more.

Although the abdication represented a bloodless revolution, the vaguely worded stipulations of the agreement reached by the former royal house and the nascent Republican government – 'The Articles for the Favourable Treatment of the Great Qing Emperor' – were ambiguous regarding the ownership and custody of the vast imperial collections and extensive imperial properties. As part of the negotiations that enabled the Beijing-based military leader Yuan Shikai (1859–1916) to replace Sun Yat-sen and install himself as president in October 1913, the new Republican government offered to treat the Qing emperor 'with the courtesies which it is customary to accord to foreign monarchs', extending to him a 4-million-tael annuity while taking control itself of the imperial court's budget.

The agreement granted the emperor, his consort the future Empress Wanrong and his family the right to reside at the Summer Palace with 600 eunuchs as well as numerous attendants and guards, and to remain in the Inner Court of the Forbidden City until their new accommodation could be prepared. The ceremonial halls of the Outer Court were to come under the control of the new government, and soon opened to the public. The seventh article of the agreement stated that the emperor's private property would be protected by the Republican government. However, it did not clarify who owned the art treasures and other artefacts in the imperial collections. The worst fears of those who viewed them as national heritage and property were realised when more than 200 objects from the Imperial Mountain Lodge at Chengde turned up in antique shops in Beijing and elsewhere.

Jin Cheng, an official of the Republic of China's Department of Internal Affairs, proposed that, in emulation of the Musée du Louvre in Paris, the government should move all of the imperial collections, including those at Chengde and Shengjing, to the Forbidden City for safekeeping under the administration of his department. He proposed the creation of a museum so that these items could be exhibited to the public. The authorities welcomed Jin's plan. Ever since the 1911 Revolution, there had been an urgent need to create institutions and mechanisms to prevent the collections of the Forbidden City and other royal establishments being sold off

22. Yuan Shikai, self-negotiated President of the Republic of China.

by the abdicated royal family and its retainers, who regarded them as their personal property. By converting the halls of the southern Outer Court of the Forbidden City into a museum, they could keep the antiquities from being claimed by anyone attempting to restore the empire, or indeed from being dispersed into overseas collections. Indeed, in the new atmosphere of national renewal, foreign interest in the Chinese arts, in particular through the agency of buyers for international collectors and museums, was seen as another form of imperial plunder of a defenceless China.

By 30 December 1913, a newly established Gallery of Antiquities (*Guwu Chenlie Suo*) had requisitioned two rooms of the Hall of Martial Valour to take receipt of the first batch of objects. The gallery was geographically positioned between two potential forces of imperial restoration: the dethroned emperor still ensconced in the northern Inner Court precinct of the Forbidden City, and the Beiyang (North China) warlords represented by Yuan Shikai, who had his headquarters at the Lake Palaces on the western side of the Forbidden City (see chapter 7). Yuan had once been loyal to the Empress Dowager, and in 1898 his swift but treacherous actions had betrayed the Guangxu Emperor who was attempting to reform the empire and brought the dowager back into the centre of power. Now, fifteen years later, Yuan, who had also enlisted the services of the influential George E. Morrison formerly of *The Times*, simultaneously filled the roles of warlord, self-negotiated President of the Republic and ultimately pretender to the throne. Ownership or custodial control of the palace collections was a powerful bargaining chip in Yuan's gamble. Also laying claim to the imperial collections was the provisional Republican government that had been established in Nanjing in Jiangsu province, the original Ming capital which had now been restored as a centre of power in competition with Beijing. It was a competition that would continue between the Nationalists and Communists from 1927 to 1949.

It took until the following year, 1914, for the Republican government to reach an agreement with the abdicated royal clan regarding the ownership of antiquities in the abandoned palaces in Chengde and Shengjing. The agreement stated that the government would purchase anything moved to Beijing from other collections for a sum to be decided by an independent assessor. Because it did not actually have the money to effect the purchase, the items were technically on loan until paid for. On 4 February 1914, however, the government published the constitution of the Gallery of Antiquities. Crates of cultural relics from north-east China destined for the gallery began to pile up in the Forbidden City.

The Department of Internal Affairs contracted the architectural firm of Curt Rothwegel from the coastal German colonial city of Qingdao in Shandong province to convert the Hall of Martial Valour into an exhibition space and build a connecting structure between it and the Hall of Tranquil Contemplation (*Jingsi Dian*) immediately behind it. The negotiation of the contract with the firm and the practical supervision of the project were entrusted to Jin Cheng. (The Hall of Martial Valour was used again for displays in the 1950s – see Chapter 1 – and refurbished and opened to the public as a gallery again in 2005.)

Many of the politicians and other individuals who facilitated the founding of the Gallery of Antiquities were primarily motivated by the need to occupy the palace space. They specifically placed the symbolically important ceremonial halls of the Outer Court off-limits to Puyi's 'little court', thereby helping to thwart any attempted restoration of the Qing – something which, during the early years of the Republic, was seen as a constant threat. The ownership of the items of the palace collections was itself a subject of contestation, but as time passed they would become valued as part of the national heritage. Major objects would now be celebrated as 'national treasures' (*guobao*), representing China's unique 'national essence' (*guocui*), just as the court language of Beijing-inflected Mandarin would become the new national language (*guoyu*), and Beijing opera, also favoured by the Manchu rulers, was to be the national form of theatre (*guoju*).

Even though the museum buildings had not yet been completed, on 10 October 1914 – the Republic's third anniversary – displays of bronzes, jades and porcelain from the imperial kilns opened to the public at the Gallery of Antiquities in the Hall of Martial Valour, the main entrance being the West Flourishing Gate. The displays were cramped, and few were labelled. In his diary the writer Lu Xun, who was an official in the Ministry of Education, noted two weeks later that the jumbled exhibits made the place look like an antique store. If press reports are to be believed, however, far more exciting for the general public was the opening of the magnificent three halls of the Outer Court (see chapter 2). For most people these represented the centre of imperial power, and access to them meant that the revolution was truly sweeping away the dynastic privileges of the past.

As Puyi was still in residence in the Forbidden City caution and deference dictated that the opening of the Gallery be low-key and given little publicity. Only government officials were invited. For some it was a 'royal museum' that had put the imperial collection on display for the first time, but it would seem that for the majority of visitors dynastic connoisseurs like Qianlong were completely forgotten. Instead, the Gallery was lauded for exhibiting the new national collection of a modern China. In this context, then, it is hardly surprising that the Gallery conveyed little idea of how royal life was lived in the Inner Court of the Forbidden City, with perhaps one small exception. The Hall of Martial Valour complex preserved the Hall of Bathed Virtue (*Yude Tang*) containing the tiled room, well, boiler and pipes of what some argued was a Turkish-style bathing facility. Apocryphal accounts hold that the Qianlong Emperor had fitted this out for his young consort from Xinjiang, the legendary 'Fragrant Consort' (*Xiang Fei*). Displayed here were items of the martial and daily attire of this imperial favourite, as well as a marble Buddha and a cloisonné brazier. A more mundane explanation of the fittings of the Hall of Bathed Virtue is that workers in a mid-Qianlong-era printery located in the Hall of Martial Valour had used the place to prepare paper.

The government also commissioned its architects to design and build a storage space for the new museum immediately to the west of the Hall of Martial Valour which was called the Building for Accumulated Treasures (*Baoyun Lou*). It was an Italianate structure that, while entirely out of keeping with the Ming–Qing architecture of the Forbidden City, did reflect the modern and international aspirations of the political masters of what was now thought of as the national collection. It was the displays in the Gallery of Antiquities – both in the Hall of Martial Valour and in the Hall of Literary Flourishing on the eastern side of the Outer

23. The Building for Accumulated Treasures next to the Hall of Martial Valour, part of the Gallery of Antiquities.

Court – that also brought modern artists and educators into direct contact with works from the Song dynasty (960–1279) that were contained in the imperial collection. Some of these paintings, produced before the 'barbarian' rule of the Jurchens of the Jin and the Mongols of the Yuan dynasties, were seen as reflecting a highpoint in Han civilisation that put it on an equal footing with anything that the West had produced. The aesthetic nationalism championed by key thinkers bolstered negative early-Republican Han Chinese views of the 'invasion dynasties' and encouraged a cultural narrowness that, in many ways, persists to this day.

In 1915, Yuan Shikai unsuccessfully attempted to restore the monarchy by declaring himself emperor. Following this fiasco, the Republican government decided to open the Gallery of Antiquities and adjacent areas of the palace to a wider public. Originally, entry to the museum had not been cheap. Scholars estimate that a 'comprehensive ticket', which allowed entry to all the halls of the Outer Court, would have cost the equivalent of one third of a Beijing commoner's monthly salary. In the first two years of operation, the policy succeeded in limiting visitors and excluding the general public; most visitors were prominent officials and citizens, or members of the city's large foreign community. However, in 1916, half-price tickets were introduced for academic groups and for the general public at festive times. Military personnel were also sold discount tickets, while students were admitted for free. At the same time the staff of the Gallery of Antiquities began to address curatorial priorities such as the preservation and conservation of objects, the maintenance and restoration of the badly dilapidated buildings of the Forbidden City and issues related to academic research and publication. They also attempted to prevent high-level officials from treating the collection as a source of gifts for eminent persons. In this, however, the officials were merely emulating the practice of the imperial family, who regularly pilfered items from the collection, asserting that they were sending objects out to be repaired but actually presenting them to retainers and others as rewards for services rendered.

On 31 May 1916, museum staff discovered that a display case had been forced open and that a number of valuable items were missing. After three guards were detained and handed over to the police as suspects, there were no more robberies for over a decade. This was in stark contrast to the situation prevailing in the imperial apartments deep within the palace, where plunder of the royal collections by all and sundry continued apace. The place was decaying around the light-fingered young ex-emperor and his favourites. Cavernous buildings and private apartments had stood unrepaired for years. The once brilliant gloss of paint on pillars, latticed windows and eves was long faded, tufts of grass grew from between the yellow tiles on the roofs and in cracks in the paving stones of the sweeping courtyards. Meanwhile, Puyi, his brother Pujie and other relatives, as well as their eunuchs and lesser attendants, devoted considerable thought and energy to purloining objects from the ancestral collection. Having learned how the new museum's inventory system worked, Puyi and his brother adroitly removed some of the most valuable items (those indicated in the inventory with five circles) to an outside hiding place when they attended lessons in the Palace for Celebrating Cultivation (*Yuqing Gong*) next to the Hall for Worshipping Ancestors. It is estimated that in this manner they, with the help of their eunuchs, spirited away between 1,000 and 2,000 highly valuable scroll paintings, albums and works of calligraphy. These were packed into more than seventy crates and shipped for safekeeping to Tianjin, in preparation for Puyi's possible escape to a more sympathetic environment.

The abdicated emperor's Scottish tutor, Reginald Johnston, and Puyi himself have documented in their memoirs how some of the other valuable treasures were purloined. In 1923, suspicious of thieves other than himself in the Forbidden City, Puyi announced that he would hold an inventory of items of the Qianlong Emperor's collection in the Palace of Established Happiness (*Jianfu Gong*), sending the eunuchs into a panic. One night the buildings burned to the ground in less than mysterious circumstances (see chapter 7). Fewer than 400 of the originally inventoried 6,643 items were salvaged. Perhaps to remove the shameful reminder of this humiliation, the emperor had a tennis court built on the site of the razed palace, once a particular favourite with Qianlong. In his mood of dudgeon, and wanting also to be regarded as a modern monarch (after all, he had by this time taken the English name 'Henry'), Puyi ordered the expulsion of 1,000 of the remaining eunuchs from the Forbidden City (excluding those who attended the imperial dowagers), bringing an end to their centuries-long involvement in Chinese politics. Not surprisingly, after leaving the palace many of the eunuchs opened antique shops in the Front Gate (*Qian Men*) shopping and pleasure district just outside the Inner City.

In his account of these turbulent years, Johnston records what an oasis the 'little court' of Puyi seemed to be:

[A]mid all the familiar scenes of turmoil, disruption, banditry,

24. The dethroned Xuantong Emperor, Puyi, on a palace roof of the Inner Court in the Forbidden City with Prospect Hill visible in the distance.

famine and civil war, the plot and stratagems of parliamentarians and wily politicians, the truculence of military adventurers and the antics of hot-headed students, there was one little stronghold in the midst of the capital which seemed to maintain itself as a haunt of ancient peace, one fragment of Chinese soil which preserved at least the outward appearance of stability and dignity, one virgin fortress in which the manners and rituals of a vanishing past still formed part of the daily routine. That home of stately decorum and tranquillity was surrounded by battlemented walls and imposing gateways that symbolised the spirit of Old China. It seemed as though that spirit had found its last sure refuge in the still mysterious halls and palaces of the Da Nei *– the 'Great Within'.*

In 1924, Puyi and the imperial family made final preparations to move to the Summer Palace in a much-delayed fulfilment of the 1912 abdication agreement. The move again raised the question of ownership of the items in the vast palace storerooms, although by this time there was little public sympathy left for Puyi or his court, especially after a failed restoration bid in 1917.

The relocation to the Summer Palace never took place. An unexpected coup by the warlord Feng Yuxiang saw Puyi and his household expelled under guard from the Forbidden City on 5 November 1925 with only a few hours' notice – the former emperor was rumoured to have been enjoying an apple while chatting with his empress Wanrong, 'Elizabeth', at the time. It is said that the imperial apartments were left in a state of disarray, with juvenile works of fiction, kung-fu novels and toys scattered all over the formerly august dwellings. Thereupon, the terms of the abdication were revised and the emperor was left with only clothing, personal items and some 'heirloom' antiques. He eventually moved to the Japanese Concession in Tianjin, where he was united with his crates of antiquities. He later rejected an overture from Chiang Kai-shek, leader of the Republic of China from 1928, who offered to re-negotiate 'The Articles for the Favourable Treatment of the Great Qing Emperor' and allow the former monarch and his court to return to the Forbidden City. The representatives of an expanding Japanese Empire, however, which had long harboured designs on the resource-rich north-east of China, had cultivated its connections with the Manchu imperial clan for many years. Now Puyi as the head of that clan took up a Japanese invitation to return to Manchuria, the homeland of his ancestors who had invaded China over 280 years earlier. In 1934, he was enthroned as the Kangde Emperor ('lasting virtue') of the Japanese puppet state of Manchukuo in its capital Xinjing (now Changchun, Jilin province).

On 6 November 1924, the day after the imperial family was ousted from the Forbidden City, the government appointed Li Yuying, a leading art historian, to chair the Committee for the Appropriation of the Qing Household which was charged with safeguarding the collection from further theft. In the following month, Li's team of specialists moved into the palace to prepare a catalogue of the royal collection. Since many of them were professors from Peking University, their students had the opportunity to become their assistants. Among them was Shan Shiyuan (mentioned in chapter 1), who described in his memoirs the appalling condition of the Inner Court as they found it. Puyi and his entourage had left many of the rooms filled with rubbish, so the cataloguers had to be careful when sifting through the midden as it sometimes contained valuable items. To prevent the scholars themselves making off with artefacts, they were required to wear dust jackets with no pockets and sleeves bound tightly by white bands. Within nine months the committee had produced a partial catalogue; it was twenty-eight volumes long and covered a large number of the estimated 1.17 million pieces in the collection.

The Inner Court of the Forbidden City was opened to the public for the first time on the Republic's fourteenth National Day, 10 October 1925. It was christened the Palace Museum (*Gugong Gongli Bowuyuan*, literally 'The Public Museum of the Former Palace'). As the museum was a 'public' (*gongli*), rather than a 'state' or 'national' (*guoli*) institution it was less generously funded than the Gallery of Antiquities. The Republican government reduced the entry fees to the Palace Museum as a way of consolidating its own waning popular support, whereas the Gallery of Antiquities still aimed to attract a more élite audience. In order to play on patriotic, anti-Manchu sentiment, the curators of the new Palace Museum were intent on preserving the palace buildings as they had been lived in by the royal family as an object lesson in Manchu decadence – presumably in the hope of putting into perspective the accusations of corruption and autocracy levelled at the current government. They also displayed to the public all the documents related to Yuan Shikai's 1915 bid to take the throne and the later abortive attempt to restore the Qing house by Zhang Xun in July 1917, one that had seen Puyi put back on the throne for less than two weeks. The inflamed Han patriotism of the early Republic gradually faded amidst the confusion and infighting of powerful interest groups. As revolutionary sentiment rose among the educated, in particular radicalising students, a mood of reverie and nostalgia also developed. Literati from the south had been attracted to university and publishing jobs in Beijing and many were profoundly moved by the decaying grandeur of the city. Famous writers and educators like Yu Pingbo, Zhou Zuoren and Lin Yutang contributed to a body of literature lamenting the passing of old Beijing and the unique culture of the Manchu bannermen – the military clansmen of the imperial house – that had created it.

The renowned scholar Yi Peiji was appointed the first curator of the Palace Museum. He managed it effectively until 1933, when he was forced to quit his post after a political rival accused him of theft and of replacing authentic objects with fakes. A rancorous and inconclusive court case ensued and Yi died a broken man. The scholar and archaeologist Ma Heng, who had served on the original cataloguing team, became director of the museum in 1933; he remained in charge until his retirement in 1954. Competition from the Palace Museum spurred the curators of the Gallery of Antiquities to devote more effort to cataloguing their entire collection. They prepared plans and maps of the Forbidden City, and allowed scholars from elsewhere in China and abroad to avail themselves of new research facilities comprising three rooms in the western wing of the Hall of Martial Valour. Although the government proposed in 1926 that the Gallery of Antiquities be integrated with the Palace Museum to form a National Museum (*Guoli Bowuyuan*), the amalgamation was resisted and only belatedly realised, in 1948.

In 1928, the warlord rulers who had controlled Beijing for many years were finally ousted from power as a result of what is known as the Northern Expedition under the command of the unified Nationalist government of the Republic. The city was now to be known once more by its early Ming dynasty name of Beiping, 'the north pacified' (see chapter 2). Finally, the Republican government in Nanjing could celebrate its control over the country. This marked a watershed in the development of the Palace Museum. To welcome the new revolutionary force there were even suggestions that the yellow-tiled roofs of the palace be painted blue, the colour of the Nationalist Party. Now, three years after its founding, the museum returned to the direct control of the Republican government. Whereas the Nationalist leader Chiang Kai-shek assumed the management of the Palace Museum, the Gallery of Antiquities came under the administration of the far less powerful Beiping Archives Preservation and Management Office of the Department of Home Affairs. Moreover, as the Gallery of Antiquities' directors had been closely associated with the defeated warlord government, financial support for the gallery was reduced and it gradually fell into decline.

In the new mood of revolutionary fervour, some left-wing thinkers like Jing Hengyi proposed selling off the palace collection and dismantling the Forbidden City itself. They argued that public ownership of the property of the former imperial house only encouraged new dynastic aspirations among the ambitious, so it would be best to dispose of everything. Such extreme views attracted little support. Meanwhile, a number of scholars were recruited to work in the Palace Museum. A board of thirty prominent individuals drawn from political, military, cultural, religious and educational circles oversaw its administration, and the government issued a set of rules of incorporation. They did this against the backdrop of continued military strife. For years the Japanese Empire had plans to expand its control of east Asia, and use the resources of China to fuel its imperial dreams. In 1931, following the Japanese invasion of Manchuria and the increased threat to Beiping, the central government ordered staff at the Palace Museum and the Gallery of Antiquities to select the most important pieces in their collections for secret shipment to Nanjing. The directors of the Gallery of Antiquities were opposed. Not only would it remove the objects from their 'power base' in Beiping but, they believed, it would signal an unwillingness on the part of the government to defend the old capital from Japanese encroachment. The authorities in Nanjing responded by bringing their agenda forward and specialists were dispatched to Beiping to oversee the controversial move.

The pre-emptive evacuation was initially carried out at night because the government did not want to alarm the population of Beiping. When word got out, though, as predicted, people took it as a sign that the government was preparing to abandon the former capital to the Japanese. Some of the museum staff travelled south to keep a custodial eye on the national treasures. Shortly before the bloody Rape of Nanjing by the Japanese in 1937, the treasures were transported west to Chongqing which would become the Republican government's wartime capital in the south-western province of Sichuan. Most of the remaining valuable items in the collections of both museums were saved from the Japanese by means of this epic 'long march'.

Other scholars remained working in the Forbidden City throughout the war. The Japanese troops refrained from pillaging the palace possibly out of consideration for Puyi, now re-throned as the emperor of their vassal state of Manchukuo, or perhaps because the heads of the Gallery of Antiquities were Japanese sympathisers. After the victory over the Japanese in 1945, the government was more determined than ever to resolve the outstanding issues of the rogue Gallery and in 1948 it was officially subsumed by the Palace Museum.

The collection of objects that had been shipped south from the Gallery of Antiquities, alone representing about one tenth of the entire imperial patrimony, was given over to the Central Museum (*Zhongyang Bowuyuan*) in the reoccupied Republican capital of Nanjing. This new arrangement would not last long. Tensions between the Republican Nationalist government and the Communist forces occupying areas in west and north-east China increased, eventually leading to all-out civil war. As this conflict unfolded in a series of titanic campaigns, the Communists renamed their Red Army the People's Liberation Army. Not long before what would be an overwhelming Communist victory in 1948, the Nationalists ordered the transportation of 852 crates containing over 600,000 of the finest items in the former imperial collection to Taiwan as part of a 'strategic retreat'.

Following the Communist takeover and Mao's proclamation of the founding of the People's Republic of China from the Gate of Heavenly Peace on 1 October 1949, the new government moved to ensure that what remained on the mainland of the collections of the Palace Museum be re-assembled and catalogued. They wanted to use the museum to enhance the prestige of the Communist Party and demonstrate how it would henceforth vouchsafe the nation's cultural heritage. Ma Heng, who had valiantly protected the collections from the Japanese and who had attempted to prevent the removal of antiquities to Taiwan by Chiang Kai-shek, remained as director. In November 1949, the government in Beijing selected the leading left-wing cultural figure and connoisseur Zheng Zhenduo to serve both as Vice-Minister of Culture and Director of the Cultural Relics Bureau. These positions gave Zheng direct jurisdiction over the Palace Museum, and he forged an effective working relationship with Ma Heng which ensured that the museum was protected and expanded in the early years of Communist rule.

During his first month overseeing the Palace Museum, Zheng prepared a preliminary report for the new premier Zhou Enlai on readying the exhibits there for display. He immediately ordered the 10,000 or so remaining crates of antiquities temporarily stored in Nanjing be returned to Beijing. In January 1950, more than a decade after their removal, the first consignment of 1500 crates arrived in the capital. However, some of the finest works from the original collection had been evacuated by the Nationalists to Taiwan, where they remained stored in mountain bunkers inaccessible to the general public for over fifteen years.

Meanwhile, the Palace Museum under Zheng Zhenduo embarked on an aggressive acquisitions policy to extend and vary what remained. Whenever possible, the museum sought to obtain items from the original collection which had been dispersed outside Taiwan. In 1950, for example, the government sent an undercover mission to Hong Kong to track down and purchase anything which had once been part of the collection. In this way, over the years the museum succeeded both abroad and in China in acquiring a large number of objects, though some were not actually from the original collection. The hunt would, and does, continue, the only hiatus being the years 1966 to 1971, when the museum was closed during the Cultural Revolution.

Another, less savoury form of acquisition is now rarely mentioned. During the early decades of Communist Party rule – even the supposedly halcyon days of the early 1950s – life in China was overshadowed by the philosophy, and practice, of incessant class struggle and the liquidation of class enemies. Individuals and families who found themselves on the wrong side of history were pressured, or forced, to donate family heirlooms to public collections. In the wave of enthusiasm for a strong and independent new China, however, many also generously handed over priceless works. They included the wealthy connoisseur Zhang Boju and his wife. Zhang continued to pursue the habit of a lifetime, but the antiquities market in Beijing was changing: the state was now the only legitimate collector. In 1957, Zhang was denounced as a 'bourgeois rightist' for making an ill-tempered observation:

> *These days, it's very difficult to find calligraphy or paintings from the Song or Yuan dynasties. Anything that's any good has either been given to the government, or else to Kang Sheng or Deng Tuo [the head of the Party's secret service apparat and deputy mayor of Beijing respectively, both of whom had a penchant for antiques]. Forget about buying anything; it's impossible to so much as set eyes on a decent piece nowadays.*

The destructive fervour of the early phase of the Cultural Revolution also acted as a smokescreen for the unscrupulous expropriation of private antiquities by the state, or at least its agents. Many rare and historically significant items found their way into the hands of Party leaders. Some of those leaders were in turn ousted as part of the constant search for reactionaries opposed to Mao Zedong's mercurial revolutionary line whereupon their 'collections' were legitimately requisitioned by the Palace Museum.

Not that the collection of the museum itself was safe from the vicissitudes of politics. In 1973, as China tentatively opened its doors to the outside world, the Cambodian ally of the Maoist government Prince Norodom Sihanouk, a man with a stately residence in Beijing's former Legation Quarter, was allowed to travel around the country. He was to be filmed for a documentary that would show a positive face of New China to the rest of the world. A devout Buddhist, Sihanouk was particularly interested in visiting the Han-dynasty White Horse Temple (*Baima Si*) outside Luoyang in Henan province. This ancient temple had been built when Buddhism was introduced from India in the first century CE. But Sihanouk's request to visit the temple sent the authorities into a panic since the place was an empty shell, having been gutted in the early years of the Cultural Revolution. Premier Zhou Enlai urgently consulted with high-level functionaries, and the prince's entourage was diverted to other scenic spots while the contents of the Buddhist prayer hall at the extensive Palace of Benevolent Tranquillity on the western side of the Forbidden City formerly used by various empresses dowager were secretly shipped to Henan in March 1973. Some 2,900 objects were requisitioned from the palace along with the eighteen statues from the Arhat Hall (*Luohan Tang*) of the Temple of the Azure Clouds (*Biyun Si*) in Beijing's Fragrant Hills (*Xiang Shan*). The Cambodians were duly impressed by the munificent collection of the recently restored White Horse Temple when they visited shortly thereafter, blissfully unaware of its provenance.

Following the Cultural Revolution, both the Palace

Museum and the Temple of the Azure Clouds petitioned to have their artefacts returned. The authorities in Henan responded that 'Zhou Enlai said the objects had been real-located [*diaobo*], and were not on loan [*jieyong*], so they don't have to be returned'. Anyway, they argued, 'the Buddhas have decided where they want to live and care not from whence they came'. In fact, the thousands of artefacts had long since been divided up between the White Horse Temple, the Henan Provincial Museum in Zhengzhou, the Henan Arts Museum and the Luoyang Municipal Museum. In recent years, these institutions have exhibited the objects around China and promoted them as 'Buddhist Cultural Artefacts from the Forbidden City'.

This story brings to mind a remark made by the connoisseur David Kidd, who lived in Beiping in the late 1940s. He revisited the city in the early 1980s to find it dramatically transformed. The multi-courtyard mansion of his wife's family at Maojia Wan had long ago become a Party compound, and for years it was the residence of Marshal Lin Biao. After touring his old haunts, or their remains, in the city Kidd observed that things in Beijing had been moved so many times that no one was sure where anything should be any more.

Despite such radical displacement, and the enforced 'loan' of museum objects to the White Horse Temple in the 1970s, today the Palace Museum boasts a collection of over 1.5 million objects, while that in Taiwan contains over 655,000 objects, including a large number of the best works from the former imperial collection. Less than 10 percent of the Beijing artefacts are on display at any one time, and the work of cataloguing continues. The collection was even larger until, in 1980, 8 million Ming and Qing dynasty palace documents (including many in Manchu) were transferred to the new Number One Archives of China. In the decade to 1959, the museum acquired 140,000 new works; by the end of 2003, post-1949 acquisitions totalled 223,506 items, of which 22,000 were voluntary and requisitioned donations from individuals received via the Cultural Relics Bureau.

Exhibits now display works of art from throughout the ages, but in the twenty-first century there has been a revival of the concept of the 'palace museum', something that was a feature of the celebrations of the museum's eightieth anniversary in 2005. More than ten semi-permanent displays focus on aspects of palace life. Meanwhile the museum continues to grow in international stature. In 2006–7, the Forbidden City hosted exhibitions from the Royal Academy in London, from Versailles and from the Kremlin. The Palace Museum's directors have claimed that it will rank alongside the British Museum, the Musée du Louvre, the State Hermitage Museum in St Petersburg and the Metropolitan Museum of New York as one of the world's top five museums – a claim also made by the National Palace Museum in Taipei, which some argue has a finer collection, one that has not suffered from political whimsy and that has for many decades been more professionally curated and displayed.

On the mainland, critics also question the way the Beijing Palace Museum is run and whether it can adequately fulfil its role as a major national cultural institution. The artist and educator, Chen Danqing, for example, has been outspoken in his derision of the much-vaunted 'museum of China'. He says it has egregiously failed to become a truly expansive national collection, one that can play a broad, civic role in the enhancement of culture and the humanities at a time of pressing need.

25. Starbucks in the Forbidden City. The western end of the Office for the Nine Ministers next to an entrance to the Inner Court. The Starbucks outlet, which opened in 2000, was forced out of the palace in July 2007 following a mass petition decrying its presence as an affront to China's dignity. The museum authorities registered 'Palace Museum' and 'Forbidden City' as brand names in the 1990s and increasingly policed the use of the brand. Accordingly, Starbucks was replaced by the state-run Forbidden City Café, which sells both coffee and Chinese tea.

While the innocuous Starbucks in the former Office for the Nine Ministers was banished in July 2007 after 500,000 people led by a prominent television personality signed a petition against it, another form of what some critics call the 'McDonaldisation of the Forbidden City' was well under way. In May 2006, the 4-hectare mazelike complex of buildings, covered walkways and pavilions at the Palace of Established Happiness destroyed by fire in July 1923 was declared open. It had been painstakingly rebuilt as a heritage project, albeit with state-of-the-art modern interiors, using Hong Kong capital. Critics lambasted the hybrid reconstruction as a desecration of the palace, and others were outraged at the announcement that it would serve as something akin to a VIP clubhouse and press centre off-limits to the general public. Many begrudged the fact that the once sternly guarded imperial enclosure was now, following its *à la mode* refurbishment, the exclusive preserve of the Party nomenklatura, museum trustees, the new rich and their foreign friends.

7

....

THREE HUNDRED YEARS ON

On the eve of his entrance to the former imperial city in March 1949, Mao Zedong famously remarked, 'Today we're heading into the capital to take the big test, no wonder everyone's nervous.' As the Communists were savouring a hard-won victory over Chiang Kai-shek's Nationalists in the 1946–9 civil war, the soon-to-be premier Zhou Enlai was also in a jocular mood. He chimed in, 'We all have to do our best to pass this next round of the imperial exams with flying colours.' Beijing was, of course, where the final stage of the traditional imperial examinations had been held, and success in them ensured selection to administer the empire. Mao added, 'If anyone has to retreat it means we've all failed. Under no circumstances can we be like Li Zicheng. All of us have to make the grade.'

This exchange followed what the historian C. P. Fitzgerald observed was the last siege of a medieval walled city in the twentieth century. It marked the 'peaceful liberation' of a city that had seemed particularly vulnerable in the face of the titanic struggle between the Communist and Nationalist armies. When another army of rebels from Shaanxi in north-west China led by Li Zicheng entered Beijing in 1644, carnage and looting followed. Three hundred years later, Mao and the Communist army had been repeatedly likened by the

Nationalists to Li Zicheng and his 'wandering bandits'. The comparison even made Mao nervous – he was well aware that Li Zicheng had only been able to hold the capital for a matter of weeks.

Mao and the Communist rebels were united with the Nationalist government and Chinese patriots of all persuasions in one thing, though: in likening the Japanese who had invaded China in the 1930s to the 'barbarian hordes' of Li Zicheng's time, the Manchus. In a long 1944 essay commemorating the events of 1644, the pro-Communist writer and historian Guo Moruo spelled out these analogies. Mao praised Guo's piece, which was better propaganda than it was history. He used it to help educate and enforce ideological discipline within the Communist Party as it was preparing to engage in a civil war for the control of China. The essay, Mao pointed out, showed how, having entered Beijing under force of arms, Li Zicheng's peasant army terrorised the population, alienated the officials of the fallen Ming dynasty and quickly succumbed to arrogance and corruption. Their undisciplined rapacity resulted in defeat, which in turn led to the successful invasion of China by the barbarian Manchus from beyond the Great Wall. Mao wrote to Guo, 'Small victories lead to arrogance, big victories even more so. They result in repeated failures. We must be careful not to make the same mistake.'

In the spring of 1644, Li, or the Marauding Prince (*Chuang Wang*) as he was also known, had triumphantly entered the imperial capital. His forces had first breached the southern walls of Beijing's Outer City (*Wai Cheng*) which dated back to the 1550s, and then overwhelmed the defences of the Inner City to launch a final assault on the Forbidden City itself. When the rebels were still at the Outer City walls, the Chongzhen Emperor ('respect order', r. 1628–44) left the palace precincts to climb the Hill of Ten Thousand Years (*Wansui Shan*) immediately north of the Forbidden City, the highest vantage point in Beijing, and one which still provides the most majestic view of the palace (see the illustration on p. 192). From there he could see smoke rising from the southern suburbs. He realised that it was only a matter of time before the invaders took the palace. He returned to the imperial apartments and, in a fit of drunken despair, tried to kill his daughters and concubines, hoping to spare them the rapacity of the conquering hordes. Fleeing the scene of his clumsy butchery, he climbed the hill once more and hanged himself from the rafters of the newly built Pavilion of Imperial Longevity (*Huangshou Ting*). By the time his body was found the invaders had terrorised the court into submission.

Later rumour claimed that the Chongzhen Emperor had in fact hanged himself from a sophora tree (also known as a scholar tree) on the eastern side of the hill. The offending tree, which was dubbed the 'criminal sophora' (*zui huai*) for allowing the emperor to die, has been replaced many times. To this day, tourists visit what is now called Prospect Hill to have their pictures taken in front of the stele marking the spot where the last Ming emperor is thought to have ended his days.

As Li Zicheng's peasant armies entered Beijing, the Ming general Wu Sangui was guarding the Great Wall against the Manchu armies pressing down on China from the northeast. The Manchus who led a coalition of forces including Mongols and Han Chinese had long nursed plans to overthrow the corrupt Ming dynasty and establish their control over the empire which they believed they had a moral, and

26. The stele on the eastern slope of Prospect Hill commemorating the death of the Chongzhen Emperor. The last ruler of the Ming dynasty hanged himself from the rafters of a pavilion on the hill on the morning of 25 April 1644.

heaven-given, right to rule. Outraged by news of the extraordinary carnage unleashed by Li's rebels in Beijing, Wu Sangui now joined forces with the Manchus to confront an army that had set out from the city under Li's command. They defeated Li's troops as they approached the Great Wall. Thereafter, Wu invited the Manchus through the Wall to allow them to help him expel Li from Beijing. Having retreated back to the city ahead of this new invading force, on 3 June 1644 Li Zicheng hastily ascended the throne in the Hall of Martial Valour and declared himself the Yongchang Emperor ('eternal fortune') of the Shun dynasty. He immediately dispatched one of his chief officers to offer sacrifice at the Altar of Heaven in the Outer City of Beijing and inform heaven that a new dynasty was in power. But the Manchu forces with their Ming allies were already bearing down on the capital. The day after Li established the Shun dynasty, he was forced to flee with his remaining men, only for them to be exterminated during a long campaign in which the Manchu-led army pursued them into western China.

The Manchus occupied the devastated city on 6 June. Instead of helping revive the fortunes of the Ming as General Wu Sangui had hoped, however, their leader the Prince Regent Dorgon declared that they would relocate the capital of their own dynasty, the Qing, from Mukden (Shengjing) in Manchuria to Beijing. Once the armies of the new Qing dynasty had pacified the city and were driving on south, the Manchus brought their newly declared six-year-old Shunzhi Emperor in royal procession through the Great Wall to take the throne in the Forbidden City. Much of the palace had been laid waste in the chaotic interregnum. As the main throne room in what would become known as the Hall of

Supreme Harmony was in ruins, the Manchu regent dealt with court business at the Hall of Martial Valour, taking up residence himself just to the east of the Forbidden City. (His princely mansion outside East Flourishing Gate was later converted into the Buddhist Pudu Temple and is now the Beijing Taxation Museum.)

Once the child emperor ascended the throne and the Qing dynasty was installed in the former Ming capital, offerings were made at the imperial altars of Heaven, Earth and the State. An edict was issued, promising the 'initiation of reform' (*dang gaige zhi chu*) and stating that 'our enterprise is nourished by renewal' (*xuan pei weixin zhi ze*). It was exactly the kind of language that would be used hundreds of years later when the Qing rulers attempted to save their floundering empire and again in the late 1970s when the Communist leaders of China launched the reform policies that 'renewed' their control and opened the country to the world. The Manchu rebuilding of Beijing began an endeavour that would eventually create the Forbidden City as we know it today.

Mao's words of caution to the Communists not to repeat the mistakes of Li Zicheng were echoed by his son, Mao Anying, when he declared, 'Gone forever is the age when the imperial families would use their power to become wealthy, the age when a minority ruled over the majority.' Although these lofty sentiments were later betrayed, Mao Anying is still extolled as the upright son of the revolutionary leader, his reputation for idealism and incorruptibility assured by his early death as a martyr on the battlefields of Korea in late 1950.

For a time the people of the ancient city were alarmed at the thought that the Communist forces surrounding them in late 1948 would repeat the destructive history of Li Zicheng's armies. Lovers of the old city like the connoisseur Zhang Boju had dark forebodings, which he expressed in an elegiac poem:

> Countless living beings,
> Capital for five dynasties,
> A thousand years of splendour.
> Pavilions and terraces that witnessed
> Song and dance
> With no thought of sorrow.
>
> Suddenly the heavens darkened,
> A gale upturned the nest,
> None escape unharmed.
>
> The pity of it!
> The ruination!
> Shed tears for our mighty land.

Cultural figures like Zhang sent representatives to help negotiate a peaceful resolution to the potentially disastrous stand off which for a time threatened to see the obliteration of the old city in violent conflict. The stalemate was resolved to Mao Zedong's advantage. Paradoxically, Zhang's worst fears would eventually be realised, not as a result of warfare, but during the restless peace of state socialism.

The new Communist rulers who now occupied Beijing were originally Spartan in their lifestyles. They were as much an occupying force as Li Zicheng's army centuries earlier. Although they had little sympathy for old Beijing or its unique culture, however, they were quick to take up residence in the imperial precinct. Zhou Enlai, who arrived ahead of Mao, immediately established himself in Zhongnan Hai (literally the 'Central and South Seas'), the Lake Palaces, previously occupied by the Nationalist general Fu Zuoyi. He oversaw the repair of pavilions and the dredging of silted lakes in preparation for Mao's entry into the city. Like the Manchus three hundred years earlier, the Communists were worried about the threat of disease. None the less, the offices and residences of the Lake Palaces offered a readymade seat of government which remains the site of China's civil and Communist Party rule to this day.

Dating from the eleventh century, the Lake Palaces are part of a garden palace complex running north to south through the heart of imperial Beijing. They had been used as an imperial pleasaunce from the time of the non-Han Chinese Jin dynasty of 1115–1234, which had established its capital there (the Qing rulers would later claim that they were the descendants and inheritors of the Jin dynasty tradition). In the early fifteenth century, the Yongle Emperor had also lived in the old Yuan palaces of the Mongols that had been built by these lakes, which he renamed the West Gardens, during the construction of the Forbidden City. The Lake Palaces were popular with later Qing rulers, too, especially Kangxi and Qianlong, and the Empress Dowager Cixi, who frequently lived there following a large-scale refurbishment of the palaces for her 'retirement' in the late 1880s. When she resumed power after quashing the 1898 reforms, her throne room and apartments there at the Hall of Ceremonial Phoenixes (*Yiluan Dian*) became the effective centre of imperial power.

After the fall of the Qing dynasty, President Yuan Shikai set up his office in the Empress Dowager's former throne room, which he had rebuilt, while he himself lived and worked in the Hall of Resident Benevolence (*Juren Tang*), a building constructed in what court chronicles called 'the Russian style', with mannered French appointments, including mock-Louis XIV mirrors, furniture and window treatments. When Yuan Shikai was resident in the Lake Palaces, he had imperial pretensions, going so far as to proclaim himself emperor in 1915. As the abdicated Qing ruler Puyi and his 'little court' inconveniently still occupied the northern section of the Forbidden City, Yuan was obliged to rule from the Lake Palaces. He renamed the area the Palace of New China (*Xinhua Gong*), with Beijing as the capital of the Great Chinese Empire (*Da Zhongguo Diguo*). As the self-styled Hongxian Emperor ('vast mandate'), Yuan prepared to ascend the dragon throne formally at the Hall of Supreme Harmony in 1916, two years after having been inaugurated there as the first president of the Republic of China. Rebellion in the provinces was to cut short his reign, which lasted a mere eighty-three days.

Daniele Varè, a long-serving diplomat at the Italian Embassy in Beijing, recalls the scene of Yuan Shikai, still president of the Chinese Republic, receiving the diplomatic body in the winter of 1914 shortly before his imperial adventure:

A little procession was coming across the ice towards us; sleighs of red lacquer and gold, with lap-robes of leopard skins; brilliant touches of colour against the background of ice and snow. Yuan Shikai was in the second sleigh. As he drew nearer the usual incongruous note became apparent. The servants who pushed the sleighs over the frozen surface of the lake wore frockcoats and tophats!

There is a large ornamental island in the lake Varè visited in 1914 called Ocean Terrace. The Qianlong Emperor favoured its many courtyards and palatial pavilions for their views and he built the Tower for Delighting in the Moon on the southern shore of the lake as an architectural counterpoint to be enjoyed from the terrace (see page 80). In the winter, from here the emperor would watch colourfully choreographed 'ice frolics' (*bingxi*). The ill-fated Guangxu Emperor may have felt differently about these famous vistas, though, for he was confined on Ocean Terrace by Cixi when she was in residence in the city. The Empress Dowager had sidelined him for supporting radical reforms in 1898 and for his lack of filial respect towards her. Today, Ocean Terrace is a scenic spot for select guests of the party-state, its buildings meticulously restored. Yuan Shikai had the Tower for Delighting in the Moon rebuilt as New China Gate (*Xinhua Men*), the main entrance to the Lake Palaces from Chang'an Boulevard. Immediately inside the gate there is a red screen wall carrying a large inscription in gold in Mao Zedong's hand reading 'Serve the People' (*Wei renmin fuwu*). Elsewhere in the Lake Palaces little of the imperial age survives. Even in the late dynastic period, the Empress Dowager ordered the construction of a number of buildings in the Sino-Western style that was to prove popular with subsequent power-holders. Energetic bureaucrats during the Republican and Communist periods razed many more of the older buildings, and the new structures exist in bizarre juxtaposition with the past.

Just north of Ocean Terrace, and immediately south of Yuan Shikai's former offices at the Hall of Resident Benevolence, stands Kangxi's Garden of Abundant Nourishment, which served as Mao's Beijing home prior to the Cultural

Revolution (see chapter 1). After Yuan's death and the subsequent years of warlord strife, in the late 1930s the Beiping municipal government established its offices in the expansive garden pavilions of the lakeside palaces. In 1928, a part of the Lake Palaces was opened to the public as a park, garden and leisure facility, and in 1933 a swimming pool was built there. However, the area was closed soon after and, following the Japanese invasion of the city in 1937, the Lake Palaces became the centre of their civilian administration.

The inappositely named Hall of Embracing Compassion (*Huairen Tang*), built near the site of the Empress Dowager's Hall of Ceremonial Phoenixes (destroyed during the foreign occupation of 1900), has also suffered repeated 'refurbishments' in its role as a venue for Party and government meetings. Featuring a meeting-hall-cum-cinema, it comprises a series of interconnected pavilions, halls, covered galleries and gardens. Party leaders have made many of their most momentous – and infamous – decisions there. On 6 October 1976, it was in one of the conference rooms here that it was decided following Mao's death the previous month to detain the 'Gang of Four', thereby bringing to an end the long decade of the Cultural Revolution. It was also here that Deng Xiaoping met with commanders of the PLA troops to commend their violent suppression of the mass protest movement on 4 June 1989.

The Hall of the Radiant Dawn (*Ziguang Ge*) lies to the north of the Hall of Embracing Compassion. Originally a pavilion from which the emperor could watch archery contests, it later served as an audience hall for receiving tribute-bearers from vassal states. It was here, in 1873, that the first accredited Western diplomats were granted an imperial audience. It is still used by state and Party officials as a reception hall for foreign dignitaries and press conferences.

The two imperial domains, the Forbidden City and the Lake Palaces, are separated by a street and the extensive courtyard houses once occupied by the Manchu nobility. But they have been jointly at the centre of real and symbolic power in China for much of the past seven centuries. Despite this, Mao Zedong refused to enter the Forbidden City. Although, over a number of days in April 1954, he walked along the perimeter of the imperial compound atop its crenellated walls from the north-facing Gate of Divine Prowess, he declined to go inside. It is said that he did not want to associate himself with the fallen Qing dynasty, or work for a new China in its thrall. Apart from frequent sojourns at Liu Zhuang, his villa on the West Lake (*Xi Hu*) of Hangzhou in south China, and at other purpose-built residences elsewhere, Mao lived a relatively austere life in the Lake Palaces until he died.

An elaborate complex of courtyard studios, pavilions, covered walkways, studies, living quarters and gardens, both ornamental and productive, makes up the Garden of Abundant Nourishment which was to be Mao's residence until 1966. The traditional courtyard dwellings are set among 1.2 hectares of gardens which had been laid out by Kangxi to emphasise the crucial role of agriculture and sericulture in the life of the empire, and to provide the scientifically inclined emperor with a place near his Forbidden City apartments in which to experiment with rice cultivation. Mao's personal quarters were in a courtyard in the eastern part of the complex called the Study of Fragrant Chrysanthemums (*Juxiang Shuwu*).

Other Party leaders were housed in spacious courtyard houses not far from Mao's quarters or in the sprawling

27. Overview of the Lake Palaces. New China Gate constructed by Yuan Shikai in the early Republican period is at the bottom of the picture. Qianlong's breakfast venue would have been nearby to the right. The island Ocean Terrace is in the middle of the South Lake. Over the bridge to the left is the Garden of Abundant Nourishment, Mao Zedong's Beijing residence during the first seventeen years of the People's Republic. Hortensia Island capped by a large Tibetan-style Buddhist *chörten* is visible in North Lake.

princely mansions of the defunct Manchu nobility scattered around the Inner City of Beijing.

In the eighteenth century the Qianlong Emperor and his successors had drunk water carted in from the Jade Source Mountain to the north-west of Beijing. Members of the imperial clans and high officials had also enjoyed speciality foods and goods not readily available to the general population. The Party revived and expanded the imperial tradition of *gongpin*, that is, the supply of exclusive foodstuffs sent to the capital under royal warrant. The socialist-era inhabitants of the Lake Palaces thus enjoyed the benefits of unpolluted water delivered through a dedicated pipeline directly from Huairou county north-east of the city. They ate organic vegetables and specially farmed meat produced under stringent hygienic conditions at Ju Shan Farm (now part of a joint venture with McDonalds). Tributary produce enjoyed by emperors and their Communist successors alike include teas like Dragon Well from Hangzhou and Houkui from Anhui, *Xiaozhan* rice, a pearly white and flavourful grain produced near Tianjin, and a myriad of other delicacies now marketed at premium prices as having been favoured by Qianlong or his predecessors. Scarcity made the system of 'exclusive provisioning' (*teshu gongying*, or *tegong* for short) an attraction for ambitious Party members. When leaders later reminded their fellows of Guo Moruo's essay on the fall of the Ming and Mao's warning about soft living and corruption, they usually did so from the luxurious pavilions and meeting halls of the Lake Palaces, or the modern conference rooms built at the Fishing Terrace State Guesthouse. It is not surprising, therefore, that the cloaked activities of the Party élite were often spoken of in somewhat sardonic terms by the older residents of Beijing as what was happening in the 'Great Within', and their children who enjoyed the enriching possibilities of a state-directed market economy were referred to as 'princelings' (*wanku zidi*). Western journalists would glibly describe the Party leaders as 'China's new emperors', but while the habits of the past cast a long shadow over the rulers of the present, the modern-style Party oligarchy is a creature born more of revolutionary privilege and economic modernisation than dynastic empire.

Jiang Zemin, who as Party General Secretary from 1989 to 2002 was a leader who enjoyed the most extravagant lifestyle of all thanks to the economic boom of the 1990s, was also aware of how divorced members of the Party leadership had become from the lives of their compatriots. Although it had always been in the interests of the Communists to isolate the Lake Palaces from the Forbidden City, the rule of the cadres clearly delineated from that of the feudal emperors, none the less Jiang was mindful of the fact that Party leaders were popularly perceived as living and working in near-imperial isolation. Shortly after the crushing of the mass protests of 1989 (a movement inspired to a large extent by widespread outrage at corruption and its fellow imperial vice of nepotism), Jiang admonished his comrades in terms that would become as standard as the rampant corruption that was overtaking the country: 'We must not cut ourselves off from the people behind high palace walls.'

The de-throned Xuantong Emperor Puyi had played tennis on a court built on the ruins of the Palace of Established Happiness. Later, Mao swam in the refurbished swimming pool of the Republican-period Lake Palaces Park and used its cabanas during the Cultural Revolution. It was here that Mao's personal 'assistant' Zhang Yufeng, a comely former train attendant from his home province of Hunan, ministered to his needs. It was also here that, in September 1971, Zhou Enlai told him that, following a thwarted assassination attempt on the Chairman's life, his close comrade-in-arms Lin Biao had taken flight to the Soviet Union and died in a plane crash in Mongolia. It was also at his poolside residence that Mao had his momentous meeting with US president Richard Nixon in the following year and where, on 9 September 1976, he finally 'went to meet Marx'.

During the Mao years, the Lake Palaces were off-limits to all but the select few. For a short period from 1977 to 1985, politically reliable tourists were allowed to visit the South Lake through the West Garden Gate, the original entrance from the Forbidden City through which Qianlong was carried in his palanquin for breakfast on 28 January 1765 (see chapter 4).

Maoist-era Beijing was re-conceived as a Chinese socialist metropolis and the capital of world revolution. It was to serve as a national model for demolition, urban renewal and reconstruction. For a time the revolutionary ideals espoused by the Party inspired the population and promised a positive political and social refashioning of the impoverished and tradition-bound nation. Former imperial precincts, already turned into public spaces during the Republican era, were now transformed into socialist leisure grounds and educational sites for the promotion of patriotism and the display of 'anti-feudal' propaganda. They were opened for mass celebrations and free 'garden outings' (*youyuan*) on key holidays such as 1 May Labour Day and 1 October National Day.

The approaches to the Lake Palaces and the roadways

leading from them to the Forbidden City were redesigned during the 1950s for both security and ease of traffic access. The most famous avenue within the Lake Palaces was over the broad marble bridge which separated the Central and South Lake compound of Zhongnan Hai from North Lake Park. This bridge, which provided one of the main roads to the Forbidden City, was now expanded into a highway. The Communists dismantled the brilliantly painted and elaborate commemorative arches (*pailou*) at either end of the bridge; their Republican predecessors had already demolished the northern wall outside the moat of the Forbidden City and its gates. In May 1956, the original northern entrance to the Forbidden City proper, the Upper Northern Gate (*Beishang Men*), which housed a ticket office of the Palace Museum from the time it opened in 1925, was torn down as part of this general road-building programme. The gate's wooden pillars constructed from the virtually extinct southern Chinese hardwood *Phoebe nanmu* were kept in storage for decades until, in 1990, they were sold off at a premium.

Directly across the road from the north-west wall of the palace was the Temple of Immense Heavens (*Dagaoxuan Dian*), a Taoist place of worship in which supplicants in the Qing dynasty beseeched the heavens for rain or snow. It was roofed with imperial yellow tiles, in accordance with Ming building conventions as it had been used by the emperor as a ritual fasting hall. The northern buildings of this compound, listed as cultural heritage properties, were converted into a printery in 1954 for the production of classified State Council and Party documents such as those recording Central Committee decisions and directives. It is now a car park and office for the administrators in charge of service personnel who work for Central Committee leaders. A strictly guarded entrance in the southern sector leads to the well-appointed cadres' club of the PLA Logistic Department.

There had been an outcry in 1903 when the original five-storey red brick Peking Hotel had been built next to the Imperial City wall, not far from Princely Mansion Well (*Wangfu Jing*) (also known in the Republican era as 'Morrison Street' in English in honour of Yuan Shikai's adviser formerly of *The Times*; today it is the city's leading shopping mall). The hotel was regarded as an invasive behemoth which loomed disrespectfully over the imperial precinct, as from its roof it was possible to see into the Forbidden City itself. In 1917, six years after the fall of the Qing dynasty, the Peking Hotel was replaced by a seven-storey building, the Grand Hotel Wagon-lits de Pékin, on the roof garden of which in the early hours of 27 June 1923, partying diplomats noticed flames coming from the north-west of the Forbidden City. A fire-fighting crew from the Italian Embassy opposite the hotel rushed to the Palace of Established Happiness complex to fight a conflagration which could easily have caused far more extensive damage. The British diplomat J. B. 'Deno' Carson and his wife Tatiana, still in full evening dress, also went to the scene to see if they could lend a hand; the emperor Puyi and his tutor, Reginald Johnston, found them there covered in ashes. Despite the Italians' efforts, the fire, which was believed to have been started deliberately by disaffected eunuchs fearful that their purloining of imperial treasures would be discovered in an audit of the royal stores initiated by Puyi, resulted in extensive losses.

Nearly fifty years later, towards the end of the Cultural Revolution, the height of the hotel would once more become an issue for China's rulers. After years of civil strife and political turmoil, the country was opening to the outside world and welcoming more tourists. An expected increase in visitors led the authorities to approve an expansion of the old Peking Hotel. A new east wing designed by Zhang Bo was to be added to the two older buildings of the hotel. Zhang, who with Zhang Dongri had designed the Great Hall of the People in the 1950s, drew up plans for a 17-storey, 80-metre-high building. But as construction workers were completing the thirteenth storey in October 1973, an urgent order came from Party headquarters at the Lake Palaces. One night Premier Zhou Enlai had noticed the lights of the building work from the government compound and realised that Mao's residence would be visible from the new high-rise. Apart from fears that an assassin might target the Chairman, Zhou and his fellow leaders were worried that foreign agents equipped with advanced technology would be able listen in to the secretive deliberations at Party central.

After much discussion and numerous meetings and remodelling, the new wing of the Peking Hotel was stopped at fourteen storeys, with an additional level set aside for utilities. For a time there was talk that the 'Five Phoenix Towers' on top of the Meridian Gate should be elevated to prevent any view of the Party compound from the hotel at all. In light of the destructive fervour of the Cultural Revolution and given the fact that all this happened at a time when China was increasingly eschewing radicalism in its dealings with the West, it was considered that such extensive new defacement of the Forbidden City would be unacceptable. Instead, Zhang Bo and his colleagues designed what they called a Screen Building (*Pingfeng Lou*) in *faux*-traditional style to be erected atop the Forbidden City's western crenellated wall. The sole aim of this ungainly new structure raised on the walls either side of the West Flourishing Gate was to block the view into the Lake Palaces from the Peking Hotel.

As the plans were being mooted, Zhou Enlai personally walked along the west wall of the Forbidden City to make sure that the Screen Building would protect not only Mao's residence and study, but also the Lake Palaces' phone exchange with its hotlines as well as his own residence and office, the West Flower Pavilion (*Xi Huating*). This 'pavilion' had been built in 1909 as a palace home for the regent Prince Chun ('the loyal', regent from 1908 to 1911) who ruled in concord with the Dowager Empress Longyu on behalf of Puyi, then in his minority. It became the site of Yuan Shikai's State Council and later a presidential palace, before being made into government offices. Despite their association with Zhou Enlai, who was all but deified following the Cultural Revolution, many of the buildings in the large compound that was the site of the socialist-era State Council were dismantled in the late 1970s when they were discovered to be of dangerously shoddy construction.

Back in the early 1950s, as the Communist Party was transforming what it regarded as the feudal, ritual-bound capital of Beijing, an English writer born in China started publishing a series of novels inspired by that very city. Just as the Forbidden City had previously fired the imaginative effusions of writers such as Victor Segalen and Edmund Trelawny Backhouse, so now Mervyn Peake's Gormenghast trilogy showed how the palace continued to have a cultural reach far beyond its walls.

Mervyn Peake was born to missionary parents in the hill

resort of Guling on Lu Shan in the southern province of Jiangxi in 1911, just as the Republican revolution was bringing an end to dynastic rule. Peake grew up in the entrepôt of Tianjin, east of Beijing, at a time when the de-throned imperial clan continued its tradition-bound routines within the Inner Court of the Forbidden City. He left China with his family in 1924, the year that Puyi was ignominiously forced out of the imperial enclave.

Peake has written that the walls, enclosures and rituals of China impressed him profoundly. When he began creating a series of novels centred on the surreal castle city of Gormenghast and the life of its seventy-seventh earl, Titus Groan, those memories came into full play. Peake's imaginary Gormenghast is built in alignment with the four cardinal points, much like the Forbidden City. It too is a city state, sprawling, half-deserted, a place described as 'a sea of nettles', 'an empire of red rust [where] rituals' footprints were ankle-deep in stone'. Its maze-like structure is also governed by a Byzantine system of laws and rituals and it is Titus's youthful rebellion against the implacable dictates of Gormenghast Law that is one of the main themes of the second book in the series, *Gormenghast* (1950). As Mervyn Peake's son Sebastian says of his father's creation, 'China is there the whole time, underlying the edifice of Gormenghast'. The young dynastic scion depicted in the book is daunted by the endless vista of pre-ordained ritual observance that lies before him as earl. He is trapped in a palatial prison:

Titus is seven. His confines, Gormenghast. Suckled on shadows; weaned, as it were, on webs of ritual: for his ears, echoes, for his eyes, a labyrinth of stone: and yet within his body something

other – other than this umbrageous legacy. For first and ever fore-
most he is child.

While it would be another decade before the deposed
emperor Puyi wrote his memoirs (his pen directed by the
steady hand of Public Security minders and the Manchu
novelist Lao She), his early years mirrored those of Peake's
fictional Titus. Puyi too felt imprisoned:

> *Every evening at dusk when all the people who had come to the*
> *palace on business had gone away a spine-chilling call came from*
> *the Palace of Heavenly Purity, the still centre of the Forbidden*
> *City: 'Draw the bolts, lock up, careful with the lanterns.' As the*
> *last drawn-out sounds of this died away there arose waves of*
> *ghostly responses from the eunuchs on duty in all the corners of the*
> *palace ... I did not dare go out of doors for the rest of the evening*
> *and felt as if all the ghosts and demons in the stories were gath-*
> *ered around the windows and doors.*

By the time Peake was writing his novels, Mao and the
Party leaders had moved into the Lake Palaces. Less than
a decade later they would convene at Peake's birthplace on
Lu Shan. There they discussed the Great Leap Forward, the
utopian mass movement launched so that China could 'catch
up with England and surpass the US' in industrial production
in the period of a few short years; China would even outdo
the Soviet Union and realise instant communism (for the
effect of this movement on the plans for the Forbidden City,
see chapter 1). But wildly inflated statistics, unprecedented
agricultural displacement and vainglorious attempts by local
Party bosses to achieve unrealistic production targets had

already led to disaster. The Party leaders gathered in the lofty and idyllic atmosphere of Lu Shan to discuss how nationwide collapse could be avoided.

Some of Mao's old associates openly opposed the excesses of the Great Leap and called on the Party to halt its murderous progress. The most outspoken of these was the Minister of Defence Peng Dehuai, who wrote what is described as a 'memorial to the Throne' (*shang shu*). For his temerity Peng was stripped of his office and put under house arrest, 'cast into a cold palace' (*daru lenggong*) and reduced to 'benighted confinement' (*you jin*).

To be 'cast into a cold palace' was imperial-era argot for being relegated to an inferior position, ignored by the emperor and his inner circle, set adrift and sequestered in an out-of-the-way part of the palace complex. Someone who had fallen from favour would be isolated so they could not reveal court secrets to others. The cold palace was friendless and ill-serviced, its luckless denizens prey to the cruel whims of eunuch servants. When discussing the 'cold palace' of internal court exile even today people quote 'The Detached Palace' (*Xinggong*), a famous poem by the Tang-dynasty writer Yuan Zhen about the forgotten court ladies of Ming Huang ('Brilliant Emperor', r. 712–56), also known as Xuanzong:

> Desolate the detached palace,
> Red flowers in lonely bloom.
> The court ladies now white-haired,
> Talking endlessly of Xuanzong.

As when the Empress Dowager confined Guangxu to Ocean Terrace, during the Communist era the Lake Palaces again became a place where favourites would be thrown into the proverbial cold palace. When the Cultural Revolution began, Mao's designated successor and the state president of China, Liu Shaoqi, was identified as the ostensible object of the purge. His extensive family compound, the Fortune of High Reward Residence (*Fulu Ju*) in the Lake Palaces, was isolated, the gates put under guard and the phones disconnected. Under house arrest a stone's throw from the Chairman's courtyard for over two years, Liu was subjected to the taunts and attacks of radical workers in the compound. In early 1967, the Lake Palaces themselves were surrounded when Red Guards manned a 'nab Liu picket' (*jiu Liu huoxian*) to force the leader to surrender. (The Lake Palaces would be the site of future mass demonstrations, too: in May 1989 during the mass protest movement and again in April 1999 when members of the Falun Gong religious sect surrounded the Party headquarters demanding recognition.) Liu's wife, Wang Guangmei, was arrested in September 1967, while he remained in neglected solitary confinement until he was evacuated to Kaifeng in Henan, where he died in 1969. Liu Shaoqi had been complicit in the consignment of Peng Dehuai to the cold palace some years earlier, the irony being that his alleged support for Peng's rehabilitation was the *casus belli* of the Cultural Revolution itself.

Mao and his supporters attacked a play written by the historian and vice-mayor of Beijing Wu Han about the outspoken late Ming dynasty official Hai Rui as being a coded plea for the restoration of Peng's reputation. They claimed that Wu, backed by Liu Shaoqi, was using the veiled language of political intrigue to present Peng as the modern-day equivalent of the upright Hai Rui. This cast Mao himself as

28. The Hall of Embracing Compassion in the Lake Palaces, rebuilt during the early years of the Republic of China and again following the founding of the People's Republic of China.

the wilful and uncontrollably suspicious emperor Jiajing, the man nearly throttled by his concubines (see chapter 2), and a ruler famous for his remark that if the peasants were restless because of onerous taxation then their taxes should be increased so they would lack the strength to rebel. The point, of course, was that in light of the great famine which followed the Great Leap, Peng seemed to have been vindicated in his criticisms of Mao – a suggestion to which the Chairman reacted with unbridled fury.

Following the Cultural Revolution it seemed for a while as though the echoes of palace intrigue were finally fading from the Chinese political stage. However, the treatment of Hu Yaobang, Party General Secretary from 1981 to 1987, puts the lie to that. Hu lived in an extensive compound adjoining the Lake Palaces, to which he gained access by a dedicated entrance. After the suppression of student demonstrators who had demanded press freedom in late 1986, Hu, who was blamed for these disturbances and other attacks on the Party, felt compelled to offer his resignation. It was accepted and he was subjected to a period of solitary self-reflection. The day this was completed and he handed over to his successor, Zhao Ziyang, he was followed through the palace grounds. As soon as he exited through the exclusive doorway it was immediately sealed up on Deng Xiaoping's order. Hu, like so many who had fallen from grace during previous power struggles, had effectively been thrown into a cold palace.

Hu's sudden death in April 1989 sparked nationwide protests. Some demonstrators who gathered at Tiananmen Square depicted Deng as an aged tyrant who, like the Empress Dowager, 'ruled from behind the screen'. Placards even appeared showing the diminutive leader dressed like the dowager. There were claims that, like her, Deng favoured cronies and was pitted against political reform. For their part, Deng and his Party supporters depicted the demonstrators as being like the anarchic Red Guards and counter-revolutionaries. In response they chose to resort to desperate measures to ensure the survival of their rule. The army was ordered to retake Tiananmen at all costs, which it did in the early hours of 4 June 1989 amidst much carnage. Hu Yaobang's successor as Party chief, Zhao Ziyang, who was accused of supporting the protest movement, was himself now 'cast into a cold palace'. Confined to his courtyard house not far from the East Flourishing Gate of the Forbidden City, Zhao died under house arrest in January 2005.

8

....

THE BANQUET OF HISTORY

On 1 April 1969, the Chinese Communist Party convened its Ninth Party Congress to celebrate the 'grand victory of the Great Proletarian Cultural Revolution'. As many Beijing wags have pointed out, it started on April Fools' Day. Just as Mao's last revolution was reaching its nadir, plans had been advanced to dismantle the Gate of Heavenly Peace. White ants had weakened the roof beams of the ancient gate and it was feared that a collapse could endanger the inviolable bodies of the Chairman and his close comrade-in-arms, Lin Biao, both of whom regularly appeared on the podium of the gate for the mass rallies that had marked the Cultural Revolution from its first public celebration on 18 August 1966.

The construction of the new Gate of Heavenly Peace in 1969–70 proceeded like so many Maoist-era undertakings, in public secrecy, the whole structure being kept under veil 'for repairs'. The rebuilding was a concrete example of Mao's well-known dicta that 'the past must serve the present, the foreign must serve China' and that 'the old must give way to the new': the wood in the eves of the new structure came from the demolition of Dongzhi Men Gate in east Beijing which had been built in 1436. When 10,000 gold-glazed *liuli*-tiles were fired for the new roof, a crucial change was made to the ancient design: the dragon motif on the original tiles was replaced with sunflowers, the botanical symbol of the masses turning to the sun-like Mao for life-giving energy. The elaborate paint work on the eaves of the new gate and the tiled roof itself were also adjusted, eliminating the decorations based on the strict code prescribed in Qing-dynasty architectural manuals for gate structures and replacing them with the design reserved exclusively for palace halls. Now in appearance, as well as in effect, the Gate of Heavenly Peace had become the equivalent of the imperial audience hall in the Forbidden City.

Work on the new gate was finished on schedule and, on 1 May 1971, Mao and other Party leaders joined the Cambodian Prince Norodom Sihanouk at tables set up with cloths, orange fizzy drinks and sweets on the podium of the gate for a special evening of fireworks to celebrate International Labour Day. When the gate was opened to the public for the first time on New Year's Day 1988 few realised that it was not the ancient Ming dynasty gateway that they were entering, but a twenty-year-old imitation rebuilt specifically for the long-dead Chairman.

Mao's evening of fireworks with the Cambodian prince would be his last public appearance. As for Lin Biao, he made only a fleeting visit to watch the spectacle, exchanging a frosty glance with the leader. Once the Chairman's hand-picked successor, the disaffected Marshal Lin was to die in mysterious circumstances only a few months later.

Mao himself returned to Tiananmen Square posthumously, and he has been there ever since. Today he is the sole resident of the square; not only does his portrait still hang on the Gate of Heavenly Peace, but his embalmed corpse lies in a large mausoleum built on the site of the Great Qing

Gate (*Da Qing Men*). It faces defiantly north, unlike all the imperial thrones and imperial sepulchres of the Ming–Qing period, whose rulers faced south even in death. None the less, over the years the granite and marble edifice where Mao lies has jokingly been referred to as 'the Fourteenth Tomb' (the Thirteen Ming Tombs are located north-west of Beijing).

The podium on the Gate of Heavenly Peace continues to be used by China's rulers when celebrations are held in the square: in October 1976, when a mass rally marked the *coup d'état* that ended the Cultural Revolution; on 1 October 1984, when a grand parade celebrated the thirty-fifth anniversary of the People's Republic (and, coincidentally, Deng Xiaoping's eighty-fifth birthday); on 1 October 1999, when Jiang Zemin officiated over a huge parade marking the fiftieth anniversary of the new China. On 8 August 2007, a carefully orchestrated public party was held in the square to mark the upcoming Beijing Olympics which were due to begin one year later to the day.

In dynastic times, much of the outward display of court ritual was one of spectacle. The Forbidden City, its approach and design were calculated to awe and impress. Its geometry was specifically aimed at directing movement, providing vistas and giving space to rituals for the rulers of the empire, its tributaries, and latterly to foreign diplomats. The palaces were also arranged to display military might. There was an archery ground near the throne rooms for competitions in martial skill. At the Lake Palaces, the Garden of Perfect Brightness and the Imperial Mountain Lodge at Chengde, large areas were designated for martial displays, sports and entertainments. In the Forbidden City, the Lunar New Year, birthdays, feast days, religious celebrations and the visits of dignitaries were all marked by buildings being lavishly decorated and with flawlessly timed rituals, the presenting of gifts and sumptuous banquets. Palace attendants silently glided through meticulously choreographed ceremonies impressing visitors with their grace and solemnity. These displays were staged to demonstrate the munificence of the throne, the benefits of the Son of Heaven's rule, and the undeniable superiority of the land of ritual and righteousness (*liyi zhi bang*). The spectacular displays were also designed to show those who were privileged to witness them that the rule of virtue could transform the world, and bring true civilisation to all.

The Qianlong Emperor, who left his mark on the Forbidden City and on Beijing more indelibly than any other dynastic ruler since the days of Yongle in the Ming, was a man who had a particular 'fascination for monumentality'. This fascination is evident in the grandiose buildings he created for his retirement in the Forbidden City, in his encyclopaedic literary projects (and his infamous literary inquisition), indeed in his tireless production of poetry and calligraphic inscriptions. Not surprisingly, he was delighted when George III sent the first British Embassy under Lord Macartney to his court in late 1793, just in time to present gifts and tribute on the occasion of his eighty-third birthday. A short dramatic work specifically adapted for the occasion was performed at the Imperial Mountain Lodge in Chengde for Lord Macartney's delectation, and education. *Peace Reigns over the Seas* was a *kunqu* opera originally designed for one of the three-tiered theatres favoured by the court. The performance featured the God of Literature (*Wen Chang*), who recites:

Our compliments to the Sage Son of Heaven, most benevolent and most filial, knower of all things and moral relations ... The ten thousand states look up in admiration at your magnificent achievements, achiever of the great plan of weaving the strands of heaven and earth. Within the four seas all acclaim your name and teachings, your benevolent influence reaches as far as the eight deserts, your kindness reaches as deep as the four extremities. There is no violent wind or excessive rain in the skies, and no waves rising from the sea. And so the country of Ying-ji-li [England], gazing in admiration at your imperial majesty, sincerely presents its tribute to the court. That country is several times further away than Vietnam. Some people have travelled from there with great difficulty for several years, and yet they have not always succeeded in reaching the shores of China. The boats of this tribute mission, however, departed in the first month of the New Year, and by the sixth month they had already reached the area around the capital. Oh Sage Son of Heaven, this is due to your benevolence and virtue reaching heaven, so the ten thousand spiritual essences are obedient to your will. If they did not have some supernatural being to escort them, how could their voyage be so swift and easy? ... Today the time has come for them to present their tributary memorial and be rewarded with a banquet.

There is a moment of drama when the creatures of the sea – the spirits of shrimp, fish, turtles, snakes and clams – are aroused. A malevolent old turtle emerges from the depths to stir up wind and waves, threatening the safe return of the barbarian tributaries. The God of Literature calls on the Dragon King himself to come to their aid and a raucous and colourful onstage battle between the denizens of the depths and the spirits of the sky ensues. The sky spirits are victorious and an urn appears on stage bearing the inscription 'Peace Reigns over the Seas' (*Si Hai Sheng Ping*), whereupon the God of Literature chants the envoi:

> *The Sage Son of Heaven in his extreme virtue has reconciled*
> *them and brought them under control, and the hundred spirits*
> *are compliant. As a result the four seas are indeed at peace.*

The harmonious world conjured up on stage for the foreign visitors did not extend far beyond Qianlong's own longevity. Indeed, it was over the seas that war, rather than peace, soon reigned.

The first decade of the People's Republic of China saw the city of Beijing once more turned into a grand capital, the setting for the spectacles of a new era. The awe-inspiring structures of imperial China were integrated into a new plan, a reorientation of the city that had Tiananmen Square at its focal point and the grand edifices of socialism on its eastern and western flanks, with the Forbidden City at its empty centre. But gradually the politics and economics of the post-Mao era changed the urban arrangement of the Chinese capital. The citizens of old Beijing had been overwhelmed by internal migrants from the 1950s; they were now increasingly displaced from the alleyway courtyards of the former Inner and Outer Cities by the new rich and relocated to tower blocks outside the fourth and fifth ring roads. In the new millennium revised city plans literally turned Beijing on its head once more. After nearly a century during which the east–west Chang'an Boulevard had increasingly been made the central feature of the city, the old north–south axis of

29. Just outside the Gate of Heavenly Peace stand two *Hua Biao*, sculpted marble pillars with small decorative cloud motifs. These 'wings' are said to represent the Board of Criticism and Protests, or the 'wood of direct speech', placed outside the imperial court for common people to write their complaints on in ancient times. The *Hua Biao* were moved further apart during the 1950s expansion of Tiananmen Square.

imperial Beijing first designed during the Yongle reign 600 years earlier was revived.

The Eternally Fixed Gate (*Yongding Men*), the original entrance to the Outer City of Beijing demolished in the late 1950s, was rebuilt in reduced version in 2004. The houses and apartments that had sprung up in the area around it were flattened to make way for a grand park that reached northwards to the Front Gate leading directly into Tiananmen Square and thence to the Forbidden City. The revived north–south axis of old Beijing was extended beyond Prospect Hill and the Bell and Drum Towers (*Zhong Gu Lou*) to the north all the way to the site of the 2008 Beijing Olympics, terminating in a serpentine dragon lake that embraced the main stadium, popularly known as the 'Bird's Nest' (*Chao*).

In 1999, a shorter parallel north–west axis had also been created which reached from the Beijing West Station northwards to the Millennium Monument located next to the Revolutionary Military Museum of China and the PLA Central Headquarters. These buildings, on the far west arm of Chang'an Boulevard beyond where the Revival Gate (*Fuxing Men*) had pierced the city wall, were in the area that Liang Sicheng and Chen Zhanxiang had once proposed as the new city centre in their "49 Scheme' (see chapter 1). Far from Tiananmen Square, a place where public celebration too readily mixed with memories of mass protest and murder, the Millennium Monument was built to usher in the new century. It is a gargantuan version of the sundials (*rigui*) that are located on short marble columns in front of the main halls of the Forbidden City. In the palace the sundials are paired with a stylised marble square grain measure (*jialiang*), and together they symbolise the unity of measurement and time within the empire.

On 1 January 2000, Jiang Zemin, then Party General Secretary and president of China, marked the new millennium by sounding the 'China Harmony Clock' (*Zhonghua hezhong*) at the monument. Bearing a legend in his calligraphy – 'China Harmony Clock, Protect for Ten Thousand Years' – the mechanism was an electronic version of an ancient tonal clock, every element of the design incorporating aspects of modern China: the number of provinces, ethnic groups, the eras of Chinese history and two side chimes representing 'peace and development'.

These days the Forbidden City is no longer derided as 'a palace of blood and tears', a place excoriated for its history as the home to China's feudal rulers who held the nation down. For over a century many of the country's leading thinkers and activists did their best to rid themselves of a culture which, they argued, frustrated modernisation. But in recent decades things long held in contempt have been touted as germane to a revived cultural landscape and sense of national identity. China's own version of what Australians call a 'black armband view of history' – that is, accounts that dwell too much on the negative events of the past – was hidden away, as an acceptable narrative of the nation presents the world with a story of 5,000 years of civilised harmony.

Since the Cultural Revolution, the Forbidden City has gradually become of central importance to the country's historical reorientation. In particular, since the late 1990s, the Manchu–Qing dynasty has been re-evaluated after having been condemned throughout the twentieth century as an alien, conquest regime that stultified China's growth and brought humiliation on the nation as a result of its internal corruption and supine dealings with the Great Powers. In

2002, a National Qing History Committee was formed in Beijing and allocated an unprecedented budget of 6 billion Renminbi to write a formal 30-million-word, 92-volume history of the Qing (making it longer than the histories of the twenty-four dynasties that preceded it combined). The earlier *Draft History of the Qing Dynasty*, compiled in the early Republican era by over 100 historians working in the former court history offices just inside the East Flourishing Gate of the Forbidden City, appeared in 1929 in 536 fascicles. The new project will produce a full draft by 2010 and, allowing for revisions, the final text will be published in 2014.

Listed as a World Heritage Site by UNESCO in 1987, the Forbidden City was the backdrop to Bernardo Bertolucci's Oscar-winning 1988 film *The Last Emperor*, in which Peter O'Toole plays Puyi's tutor Reginald Johnston. The success of that film came at a time when the Palace Museum was learning to market itself, and it had a profound impact on how this was done. Thirty-three international exhibitions have been mounted by the Palace Museum in the three decades since 1974. Although known as the Former Palace (*Gugong*) in Chinese, it is the éclat of the exotic, secretive and unknown that is used to promote the place overseas. The mystique of court life, as well as the stories and works of the great Qing emperors, even the controversial figure of the Empress Dowager, are now used to sell China.

The palace is celebrated as the Forbidden City, *Kaiserpalast*, *Verbotene Stadt*, *Cité interdite*, *Shinkinjō*, *Verboden Stad* and *Cidade Proibida*. The language used in the catalogues produced to accompany the export exhibitions further adds to the allure of past grandeur. It is variously described as palatial, majestic, mysterious, rich, prized, splendid, exquisite, unique, priceless, exotic, precious, inexhaustible, extraordinary and sublime. And the statistics relating to the Forbidden City form a constant refrain: 72 hectares in area, with over 900 rooms and more than 1 million objects. Although the Forbidden City has been physically absent from the international displays its presence looms large.

The Forbidden City was the real star of Bertolucci's film, but it was not until a production of Giacomo Puccini's opera *Turandot* in the late 1990s that it became the site for the kind of spectacle that had not been witnessed there for nearly a century. The show was staged by the Florence-based Opera on Original Site, Inc., a company which specialises in on-site performances, having previously performed *Aïda* at Luxor, Egypt. *Turandot* was years and, the producers boasted, US$15 million in the making. The orchestra was conducted by the renowned Zubin Mehta and the opera set was designed by Zhang Yimou, the director of films like *Raise the Red Lantern* (1991) and *Shanghai Triad* (1995). The cultural mega-event was not, however, merely a contemporary example of the kind of ping-pong diplomacy made famous in the early 1970s when sport opened the door for China's re-entry on to the world stage. Rather, it was a grandiloquent gesture which, in consideration of the names of the courtiers in Puccini's work, featured Ping, Pang and Pong marketing that had the money flowing in.

The promoters claimed that the show would be in the Palace of Heavenly Purity, the main hall of the Inner Court of the Forbidden City. 'The old palace', their press release announced, 'housed the Emperor's bedroom, but later the rooms were used for royal audiences – foreign ambassadors were received here, attended on occasion also by the Empress.

中国人民伟大的无产阶级革命家、杰出的共产主义战士周恩来同志永垂

30. 'May the Outstanding Proletarian Revolutionary of the Chinese People, the Great Communist Warrior Comrade Zhou Enlai Live Forever!' The state funeral for Zhou Enlai held at the Ancestral Temple, January 1976.

The last royal ceremony to take place here was the wedding of the last Chinese Emperor Puyi, in December 1924 [it was actually in 1922].' Having paid for tickets which ranged in price from a few hundred to over a thousand US dollars, patrons would watch this once-in-a-lifetime production in the palatial compound 'surrounded by gardens [that] used to be a meeting place of noblemen and an imperial audience venue for the Emperor in past times'. In fact, the lavish performance was set up in the extensive courtyard of the Ancestral Temple (*Tai Miao*), the notional graveyard for the imperial dead, just outside the precincts of the Forbidden City – it would have been inauspicious to have it located inside the sacred city itself.

The final production – grand, over-designed, lavishly costumed and with its rent-a-crowd PLA cast – was called by one reviewer 'long on style short on substance'. It was neither commercially nor culturally successful. However, this did not stop the PBS TV network from making an earnest documentary about it. Nor did it prevent the lighting director of the show, Guido Levi, from commenting sardonically on the gimmickry of using Zhang Yimou to mount the show in Beijing as 'a vulgarity I find monstrous'.

The Ancestral Temple first opened to the public in 1924 following the expulsion of Puyi's 'little court' from the Forbidden City. After the Communist occupation of Beijing, it was renamed the Beijing Municipal Workers' Cultural Palace and was converted into a public park which opened on International Labour Day 1950. Guo Moruo, the Maoist-era lackey literatus whose calligraphy adorns the northern entrance to the Forbidden City, wrote a poem to mark the occasion in which he gushed, 'Temple of emperors past, cultural palace for the present'. On 12 May 1950, the first public art exhibition was held there: a display of photographs of the labouring people of the fraternal socialist country of Romania.

While the grounds of the temple would become a popular leisure park, for the first decades of the People's Republic the main building was used, like the Hall of Columns at the Kremlin in Moscow, to display the bodies of dead state and Party leaders for ritual mourning. The Ancestral Temple was first employed for this purpose in October 1950, when over 10,000 people lined up to view a catafalque surrounded by flowers displaying the open coffin of Ren Bishi, the recently deceased Secretary of the Central Government of the new People's Republic. Over the years the remains of eight senior Party leaders were put on display in the Ancestral Temple before being disposed of at Babao Shan, the state crematorium and columbarium west of the city. The last Party leader to receive the honour was a man whose own history had been closely involved with the Forbidden City, Zhou Enlai, who died on 8 January 1976.

A quarter of a century later, another requiem was to be held there. In 2002, a mock funeral was staged at the Ancestral Temple for the satirical film *The Player* (*Da Wan'r*), directed by Feng Xiaogang. This time it was for the dead boss of the Hollywood-based Player Film Company, played by Donald Sutherland (particularly popular with local audiences for his famous portrayal in the 1977 film *Bethune* of the saintly Canadian Communist doctor Norman Bethune, who died during the war while treating wounded Party soldiers and was subsequently extolled by Mao for his spirit of self-sacrifice). The funeral at the Ancestral Temple in *The Player* is an outlandish affair featuring performances by stand-up comics, arias from

Beijing operas and crooners singing popular songs. The show bids farewell to the dead boss while at the same time providing an in-your-face advertising opportunity for his company.

The imperial centre has provided a backdrop for the work of other colleagues of Zhang Yimou. They include Tian Zhuangzhuang, who features breakdancers strutting their stuff at night in front of the Meridian Gate in his 1988 film *Rock 'n' Roll Youth*. Popular around the time of the 1989 protest movement, the film is based on a story by the PLA writer Liu Yiran. Its main character is a bit of a tearaway frustrated with his love life, the Party and social control. One night, he decides he needs a real party:

I head for the Meridian Gate to spend the evening. A good night there is just incredible, all of China's break dance élite in one place. They're all 'problem youths' ... Can't hack their parents, can't deal with the traditional love scenario, hate their bosses. They all go there to cut loose. What could be better: dancing to rock music where the old Qing emperors slept. It's a real turn-on ...

When I reach the Meridian Gate the place is exploding with break dancing. Rock music hits me on all sides: ghetto blasters of every shape and size on the ground, stuck on the back of bikes, hung in the trees. Sorry, Your Imperial Highness, we couldn't be bothered to prostrate ourselves on the ground, kowtow, and cry out 'Ten Thousand Years' tonight. Instead, our thunder is shaking you from your dreams ...

In 1990, Tian Zhuangzhuang made another movie – this time about Li Lianying, the Empress Dowager's chief eunuch. In the last scene of that film the aged Cixi expires while being carried by Li, and he collapses under her weight.

Many regarded it as a political allegory with contemporary significance.

Over twenty years earlier young people had staged a different kind of party at the Meridian Gate. In June 1967, Red Guards had held a mass performance in the forecourt of the Forbidden City to celebrate the twenty-fifth anniversary of the publication of Mao's *Talks at the Yan'an Forum on Literature and Art* which had become the basis of all cultural activity in the People's Republic. Thirty-five years later, in June 2001, under another Party leader, Jiang Zemin, 30,000 people crammed into the forecourt to listen to a performance by the Three Tenors – Luciano Pavarotti, Placido Domingo and José Carreras – who had been invited to China as part of the charm offensive to woo the International Olympic Committee and secure the 2008 Olympic Games for Beijing. At an official reception for the singers in the Lake Palaces headquarters of the Communist Party Jiang Zemin sang 'O Sole Mio' with Pavarotti who later opined that Jiang could have been a great opera singer if he had only chosen to concentrate on music.

In the pavilions on Hortensia Island (*Qionghua Dao*) in North Lake Park, there is today a restaurant called Emulating the Imperial Table (*Fangshan Fanzhuang*), founded in 1925 by former chefs from the Forbidden City. In the late 1950s, Zhou Enlai declared it to be a 'national treasure' and had it moved from the northern shore of the lake on to the island where it could more easily be used to entertain not only visiting dignitaries but also Party leaders, many of whom lived close by in the Lake Palaces or in princely mansions in the old Inner City. Nowadays, it has been refurbished in the popular style of red and gold imperial gaud. Private dining rooms are elaborately furnished with satin couches and divan-like opium

31. Looking towards Hortensia Island at the North Lake from the Five Dragon Pavilions on the north shore of the lake. An entrance in the middle of the covered walkway now leads to the restaurant Emulating the Imperial Table.

beds and patrons are encouraged to be emperor or empress for a meal. The chefs offer dishes that imitate dynastic ostentation at suitably inflated prices.

The Manchu–Han Complete Banquet was developed over many years in the Qing dynasty. When Kangxi and Qianlong travelled south on their tours of inspection they were fêted with the finest foods and delicacies wherever they went (see chapter 3). Upon returning to Beijing they would have their favourite new dishes added to the imperial menu of the Forbidden City. According to the chefs at Emulating the Imperial Table a full Manchu-Chinese Complete Banquet would have taken three days to serve. Today, there are six versions of the banquet, ranging in price from the mildly expensive to the exorbitant. More run-of-the-mill dishes popular with visitors include Duck Webs in Goldfish Shapes, Frog-like Abalone, Sweet-pea Gelatin Cubes, Corn Flour Dumplings and Cold Fish Maw Wrapped in Egg Skin. They are touted as having delighted the palates of the last emperors.

The famous twentieth-century writer Lu Xun, mentioned earlier, once remarked that China itself was like a banquet, one at which foreigners from all over the world were anxious to gorge themselves. It is an observation that has inspired, and annoyed, many thinkers and politicians ever since. Lu Xun also spoke of the unsettling ability of Chinese culture to transform and homogenise anything that came within its thrall. He called it a soysauce vat (*jianggang*) that darkened anything, or anybody, that entered it. After the high-revolutionary era of Mao Zedong, many people would wonder whether a radical new enterprise that had aimed to transform the country for the better had not been fatally tainted by the soysauce vat.

32. 'The Forbidden City in the Moonlight', by Wang Aihua, 1976. Wang belonged to the No Name artists of Beijing who produced lyrical work throughout much of the Cultural Revolution. One of the many noteworthy and moving works produced by the group was a painting made of Chang Ling, the tomb of the Yongle Emperor, founder of modern Beijing. It was painted by Zhou Wenliang on 18 August 1966, the day that Mao Zedong reviewed the first Red Guard rally at Tiananmen Square, an event with which this book begins.

During a short-lived period of de-Maoification after 1978, the Sichuan poet Sun Jingxuan echoed Lu Xun's sentiments in his poem 'A Spectre Prowls Our Land':

> ... Have you seen
> The spectre prowling our land?
>
> You may not recognise him,
> though he stands before your eyes,
> For like a conjurer,
> master of a never-ending transformation,
> One moment in dragon-robe of gold brocade
> He clasps the dragon-headed sceptre,
> The next in courtier's gown
> He swaggers through the palace halls;
> And now – behold – a fresh veneer!
> The latest fashion! And yet
> No mask, no costume, no disguise
> Can hide the coiled dragon
> branded on his naked rump ...
>
> China, like a huge dragon, gobbles all in its path,
> Like a huge vat, dyes all the same colour.
> Have you not seen the lions of Africa,
> the lions of America,
> Fierce kings of the jungle?
> When they enter our dragon's lair
> they become mere guard-gods,
> rings through their pug nostrils,
> standing guard at yamen and palace gate ...

In 1996, the year before the resumption of Chinese suzerainty over Hong Kong, a territory lost by the Qing court over 150 years earlier, the poet Leung Ping-kwan wrote a meditation on the return of his home town to the embrace of a China in resurgence. His 'Cauldron' is a vessel for dynastic pretension, one that serves an empty imperial banquet. In the age of a revitalised, much transformed, Beijing his poem is a fitting epitaph for the Forbidden City – at once monument to the dark power of the past, to the 'tintinnabulations of history', but also the exquisite embodiment of a grand tradition that could one day inspire a new 'arabesque of beauty':

As the Zhou Dynasty rebuilt the Empire
and celebrated the unity of All-Under-Heaven,
courtiers were honoured, ceremonial music composed,
metals melted, vessels cast, new injunctions set in bronze,
power revalidated.
The grand banquet commenced, noblemen and elders took
the places of honour;
while savage fauna bubbled restlessly in the cauldron,
a sober phoenix motif replaced the gruesome mask of the
Beast.

Our humble bellies have ingested a surfeit of treachery,
eaten their fill of history, wolfed down legends –
and still the banquet goes on, leaving
an unfilled void in an ever-changing structure.
Constantly we become food for our own consumption.
For fear of forgetting we swallow our loved ones,
we masticate our memories and our stomachs rumble
as we look outwards.

Creation's aspirations are trussed,
caught tight by the luminous bronze.
In his campaign against the Chu, the southern state,
as the Emperor approached the wilderness beyond the
Central Plain,
ten thousand bawled for the rustics beyond the pale,
to make their low bow of homage;
stone and metal engraved; vessels fashioned;
tintinnabulations of history.

The proclamations sit heavy on the stomach,
destroy the appetite;
the table is altogether overdone.
May I abstain from the rich banquet menu,
eat my simple fare, my gruel, my wild vegetables,
cook them, share them with you?
Is there a chance
your pomp and circumstance could ever change,
evolve
slowly
into a new motif,
some new arabesque
of beauty?

33. The Palace Museum seen from Prospect Hill. A photograph taken by Hedda Hammer (Morrison), resident in Beiping 1933–1946. The Upper Northern Gate of the Forbidden City, demolished in 1956, is visible in the foreground.

MING AND QING RULERS

Only rulers – emperors, empresses, empresses dowager, regents and pretenders – mentioned in the book are listed here. The reign title is followed by the personal name of the emperor. The Ming rulers were all surnamed Zhu; thus the Yongle Emperor's name was Zhu Di. The Qing emperors who ruled in Beijing were of the Aisin Gioro clan. Thus the full name of the last Qing ruler, the Xuantong Emperor, was Aisin Gioro Puyi.

MING DYNASTY (1368–1644)

Hongwu ('abundantly martial'), Zhu Yuanzhang, r. 1368–98

Jianwen ('establishing the civil'), Zhu Yunwen, r. 1399–1402

Yongle ('perpetual happiness'), Zhu Di, r. 1403–25

Xuande ('proclaimed virtue'), Zhu Zhanji, r. 1426–36

Jiajing ('vast serenity'), Zhu Houcong, r. 1522–67

Wanli ('broad vision'), Zhu Yijun, r. 1573–1620

Tianqi ('heavenly awakening'), Zhu Youjiao, r. 1621–7

Chongzhen ('respect order'), Zhu Youjian, r. 1628–44

QING DYNASTY (1644–1911)

Tianming ('heavenly mandate'), Nurhaci, r. 1616–26

Tiancong ('heavenly direction'), Hong Taiji, r. 1627–35 as Khan, or ruler, of the Latter Jin dynasty

Chongde ('respect virtue'), Hong Taiji, r. 1636–43 as emperor of the Qing dynasty

Prince Dorgon (younger brother of Hong Taiji), regent, 1643–50

Xiaozhuang (Borjit Bumbutai), empress and later empress dowager, 1613–88

Shunzhi ('favourable sway'), Fulin, r. 1644–61

Oboi, Guwalgiya clan, regent, 1661–9

Kangxi ('lasting prosperity'), Xuanye, r. 1662–1722

Yongzheng ('concord and rectitude'), Yinzhen, r. 1723–35

Qianlong ('enduring glory'), Hongli, r. 1736–95

Jiaqing ('vast celebration'), Yongyan, r. 1796–1820

Daoguang ('glory of right principle'), Minning, r. 1820–50

Xianfeng ('prosperity for all'), Yizhu, r. 1851–61

Cixi ('benevolent and auspicious'), Yehonala clan, empress dowager, co-regent 1861–72, co-regent 1875–81, regent 1882–7, and again as 'mentor in state affairs' 1898–1908, d. 1908

Ci'an ('benevolent and tranquil'), Niuhulu clan, empress dowager, co-regent, 1861–72, 1875–81, d. 1881

Prince Gong ('the respectful'), Yixin, brother of the Xianfeng Emperor, regent, 1861–73, d. 1898

Tongzhi ('joint rule'), Zaichun, r. 1862–74, as Qixiang ('auspicious felicity') in 1861

Guangxu ('glorious succession'), Zaitian, r. 1875–1908

Longyu ('boundless plenty'), Yehonala clan, niece of Cixi and empress of the Guangxu Emperor, empress dowager, regent, 1908–11, d. 1913

Xuantong ('proclaimed continuity'), Puyi, r. 1909–11, aka 'Henry', d. 1967. Upon his expulsion from the Forbidden City in 1924, Puyi formally relinquished his reign title. He later took the throne in Manchukuo under the reign title Kangde ('lasting virtue'), 1934–1945

Wanrong ('fair countenance'), Gobulo clan, aka 'Elizabeth', empress of Puyi, 1922–46, d. 1946

Prince Chun ('the loyal'), Zaifeng, regent, 1908–11, d. 1951

NON-DYNASTIC

Yongchang ('eternal fortune'), Li Zicheng, 1606?–45, of the short-lived Shun dynasty in 1644

Hongxian ('vast mandate'), Yuan Shikai, 1859–1916, self-proclaimed emperor of the 83-day Great Chinese Empire in 1916

GLOSSARY

The names for buildings in the Forbidden City and the Lake Palaces are confusing. A full glossary of buildings and terms used in this book can be found online at <www.chinaheritageproject.org/theforbiddencity>.

Cheng: a crenellated wall or keep. Until the 1910s, Beijing had a number of such walls, often called 'cities' in English. There was the Outer City (*Wai Cheng*), around the southern suburbs, the Inner City (*Nei Cheng*) inside of which was the Imperial City (*Huang Cheng*), which in turn surrounded the Forbidden City (*Zijin Cheng*). The Great Wall is simply a 'long wall', or *chang cheng*.

Chu: literally 'place' or 'location', also often 'office' as in the Office of Military Intelligence (*Junji Chu*).

Dian: originally meant a high-ceilinged hall. It later came to be used for imperial/royal audience halls, the dwellings of emperors and empresses and for Taoist and Buddhist halls of worship.

Fang: room, or place in charge of palace services, such as the Office of Respectful Service (*Jingshi Fang*).

Fu: residence or large administrative body, such as the Imperial Household Department (*Neiwu Fu*).

Ge: room or pavilion, usually of two or more storeys. As in the three-storey opera theatre the Pavilion of Delightful Melodies (*Changyin Ge*).

Gong: palace. Originally the word for a house or building, it was later reserved for palaces where official business was conducted by the emperor or where he or his empress and consorts lived. In the Forbidden City many of the imperial residences (*Qianqing Gong, Chuxiu Gong*, and so on) are 'palaces'. It is also used for some temples. Interestingly, the Qing emperors' main residence in the Forbidden City was a 'hall' (*dian*): the Hall of Mental Cultivation.

Guan: a small hall, as in the Azure Cloud Hall (*Cuiyun Guan*).

Hai or *haizi*: literally 'sea'. The lakes of Beijing are called 'seas' – thus the Lake Palaces of Zhongnan Hai and Bei Hai are literally the Central, South and North Seas. They are connected to a series of other lakes further north such as the Anterior Lake (*Qian Hai*) and Posterior Lake (*Hou Hai*).

He: river or moat, as in the Forbidden City moat (*Hucheng He*) or the River of Golden Waters (*Jinshui He*), one branch of which runs in front of the Gate of Heavenly Peace, while another runs between the Meridian Gate and the Gate of Supreme Harmony within the Forbidden City.

Ju: literally 'residence', a poetic name for a dwelling or place of work.

Ling/Lingqin: imperial tomb or mausoleum, with a 'subterranean palace' or *di gong*. For princes and consorts there were *yuanqin*.

Lou: tower, often a pavilion built on top of another structure, such as the Five Phoenix Towers (*Wufeng Lou*) on the Meridian Gate.

Men: gate or door. From the majestic palace gates to the more common doorway of a domestic residence.

Miao: a temple or place for sacrifice. As in the Ancestral Temple (*Tai Miao*) outside the south-east wall of the Forbidden City.

Shan: a hill, mountain, hillock or col. Prospect Hill (*Jing Shan*) is a *shan*, as are the Fragrant Hills (*Xiang Shan*) to the west of Beijing.

Shi: a room.

Si: temple, as in the Temple of the Azure Clouds (*Biyun Si*).

Suo: a small and restricted courtyard, or a place for official business such as the Office for the Nine Ministers (*Jiuqing Suo*).

Tan: an altar. *Tian Tan* is the Altar of Heaven, often mistakenly referred to as the Temple of Heaven.

Tang: hall, study or room. Although this could indicate a pavilion-like structure, it is often used in the titles of personal studies or studios. Thus Qianlong's Room of the Three Rarities (*Sanxi Tang*).

Ting: pavilion, often with open sides.

Xinggong: detached or travelling palace. The Fishing Terrace (*Diaoyu Tai*) to the west of the walled city of Beijing was a *xinggong*.

Xuan: loggia or studio. A structure surrounded by open galleries or walkways such as the Studio of Convivial Delight (*Tongyu Xuan*).

Yuan: a garden, from the most intimate space or small decorative gardens inside the Forbidden City to the extensive garden palaces that were built to the north-west of Beijing during the Qing dynasty.

Zhai: a studio, the study of a man of letters; also a larger space for leisure, such as the Studio of Exhausted Diligence (*Juanqin Zhai*), which contains a theatre.

VISITING THE FORBIDDEN CITY
AND IMPERIAL PROPERTIES

THE FORBIDDEN CITY

There are two entrances to the Forbidden City for the general public. The main, southern entrance is through the original front portal, the Meridian Gate (*Wu Men*), and the other through the Gate of Divine Prowess (*Shenwu Men*), located at the north end of the palace inside the moat. You can also approach the Meridian Gate courtyard from either the east or the west by a picturesque route which follows the course of the moat alongside the palace's crenellated walls.

To appreciate the immense scale of Beijing during the height of the Ming dynasty, however, begin your journey at the recently reconstructed Eternal Fixed Gate (*Yongding Men*), located on the South Second Ring Road. This is the starting point of the 8-kilometre north–south axis of the old city. A pedestrian walk has been laid out from this gate to the Front Gate (*Qian Men*) of the Inner City. The walkway takes the visitor past the Altar of Heaven (*Tian Tan*) on the east with its magnificent blue-tiled Hall of Bountiful Harvests (*Qinian Dian*), and the Altar of the First Farmer (*Xiannong Tan*) on the west, where prayers were offered for good harvests. (The latter is now a sports ground.)

From the Front Gate, walk around the Mausoleum of Chairman Mao (*Maozhuxi Jinian Tang*), sometimes open to the public. (Long queues indicate that it is.) Continue north through Tiananmen Square past the Monument to the People's Heroes (*Renmin Yingxiong Jinian Bei*), and go through the underpass crossing Chang'an Boulevard to the Gate of Heavenly Peace (*Tiananmen*) itself. Walking through the portal over which Mao's portrait hangs, you enter what was once the Imperial City (*Huang Cheng*) that itself once enclosed the Forbidden City, the Lake Palaces and the residences of the nobility surrounding them. To the west of the gate is Zhongshan Park (called Central Park in the early Republic), formerly the Altar of State (*Sheji Tan*), also known as the Altar of Grain and the Earth. To the east lies the Ancestral Temple (*Tai Miao*) mentioned in chapter 8.

If you continue north through the Gate of Heavenly Peace, you will pass through the Gate of Rectitude (*Duan Men*) into the vast forecourt of the Forbidden City itself. Entering the Forbidden City or Palace Museum through the Meridian Gate you can ascend the gate by the stairs to the left and enjoy the views from the parapets. The Hall of Martial Valour (*Wuying Dian*) to the west of the first courtyard of the palace, through which runs the River of Golden Waters (*Jinshui He*), was the site of the first museum created after the fall of the Qing dynasty, the Gallery of Antiquities (*Guwu Chenlie Suo*) (see chapter 6), now a well-appointed gallery. Next to it stands the European-style Building for Accumulated Treasures (*Baoyun Lou*).

The Palace Museum itself contains numerous exhibition halls in the galleries and courtyards of both the Outer and Inner Court (*Wai Chao* and *Nei Ting*). Details of the current and permanent exhibitions are provided in the map you are given when you buy a visitor's ticket. In accordance with tradition, the Forbidden City is divided as follows:

The Central Route (*Zhong Lu*), which takes the visitor to the three main audience halls in the Outer Court (*Wai Chao Zhong Lu*) and the three halls in the Inner Court (*Nei Ting Zhong Lu*) immediately to their north.

The Eastern Route of the Outer Court (*Wai Chao Dong Lu*), the 'civilian precinct' of the palace which includes the offices of the Grand Secretariat (*Nei Ge*) and the Hall of Literary Flourishing (*Wenhua Dian*).

The Eastern Route of the Inner Court (*Nei Ting Dong Lu*), which contains some of the northern residences still closed to the public, including some of the Eastern Six Palaces (*Dong Liu Gong*) and two of the main permanent exhibitions – of imperial clocks at the Hall of the Ancestors (*Fengxian Dian*) and of antiquities.

The Outer Eastern Route of the Inner Court (*Nei Ting Wai Dong Lu*), which features the 'miniature Forbidden City' built for the Qianlong Emperor's retirement. This contains an extensive garden and apartments used by the Empress Dowager Cixi as well as the infamous 'Pearl Consort well'.

The Western Route of the Outer Court (*Wai Chao Xi Lu*), the 'martial precinct' which includes the Hall of Martial Valour, the original site of the Gallery of Antiquities.

The Inner Western Route (*Nei Ting Xi Lu*) of the

Inner Court, which takes the visitor to the main residence of the emperors, the Hall of Mental Cultivation (*Yangxin Dian*), and the courtyard apartments of the Western Six Palaces (*Xi Liu Gong*), or imperial seraglio, that lie behind it.

The Outer Western Route of the Inner Court (*Nei Ting Wai Xi Lu*), which includes some magnificent courtyards used by senior imperial wives and empresses dowager, none of which are open to the public.

From either the Inner Western or Inner Eastern Route the visitor enters the Imperial Garden (*Yuhua Yuan*) in the central northern precinct of the Forbidden City which contains on its western side the Studio for Cultivating the Heart (*Yangxin Zhai*), the building that the last emperor Puyi gave over for the use of his Scottish tutor Reginald Johnston.

PROSPECT HILL

Leaving the Forbidden City from the northern entrance, the Gate of Divine Prowess, the visitor should continue north to visit Prospect Hill (*Jing Shan*) from which the best views of the Forbidden City can be had. On the eastern side of the hill there is a stele commemorating the Chongzhen Emperor, last ruler of the Ming dynasty, who killed himself when the city was invaded in 1644.

THE LAKE PALACES

Leaving Prospect Hill by the western exit, the visitor can go into the North Lake Park (*Bei Hai*) by its eastern entrance.

Crossing the marble bridge to Hortensia Island (*Qionghua Dao*), which is crowned by a large white Tibetan-style *chörten*, the visitor can then walk along the covered corridors on the northern edge of the lake to Emulating the Imperial Table restaurant (*Fangshan Fanzhuang*) which serves mock-imperial cuisine (see chapter 8). Around the lake's northern bank are temples and studios, including the Studio of the Quiet Heart (*Jingxin Zhai*), where the Empress Dowager would often take lunch and where she enjoyed practising calligraphy and painting. In the late 1880s, the Empress Dowager had a railway constructed which linked her residence in the Lake Palaces to this studio. To avoid assailing the dignity of the palace, however, she had the locomotive discarded and instructed eunuchs to pull the carriages. North Lake Park is the only part of the extensive Three Lakes of the West Gardens (*Xi Yuan San Hai*), or the Lake Palaces, open to the public. To the south lie the Central and South Lakes (*Zhongnan Hai*), the headquarters of the Chinese Communist Party and the seat of government of the People's Republic of China.

The above itinerary from the Eternal Fixed Gate to North Lake Park can be traced using Google Map (<www.googlemap.com>).

THE GARDEN PALACES

The Forbidden City is at the centre of a complex of palaces that were used by the emperors of the Qing dynasty. To fully appreciate the nature of imperial life during the height of the dynasty in the seventeenth and eighteenth centuries, the visitor should be sure to see the other imperial garden residences and parks of Beijing: the Summer Palace (*Yihe*

Yuan), the Ruins of the Garden of Perfect Brightness Park (*Yuanming Yuan Yizhi Gongyuan*) and the Fragrant Hills Park (*Xiangshan Gongyuan*), all to the north-west of the city. The Temple of Ten Thousand Longevities (*Wanshou Si*), on the West Third Ring Road, was used as a waystation by the Empress Dowager when she travelled to the Summer Palace from Beijing by royal barge. Jade Source Mountain (*Yuquan Shan*), located between the Summer Palace and the Fragrant Hills, is a restricted Communist Party retreat. The Kangxi Emperor's garden palace, Garden of Delightful Spring (*Changchun Yuan*), to the west of what is now Peking University, was destroyed in 1860 by an Anglo-French expeditionary force following the Second Opium War.

THE MOUNTAIN LODGE, SHENYANG AND PUYI'S PALACE

Other major Qing imperial sites are the extensive walled Imperial Mountain Lodge (*Bishu Shanzhuang*) at Chengde in Hebei province, approximately 160 kilometres north-east of Beijing, and the Shenyang Palace Museum (*Shenyang Gugong Bowuyuan*) in the provincial capital of Liaoning (formerly Shengjing, or Mukden, the original capital of the Qing). Up until the late 1820s, Qing emperors undertook 'tours of the east' (*dong xun*) to visit the Manchu homelands outside the Great Wall. There is now a highway to Chengde, and buses as well as trains regularly depart from the main Beijing Railway Station. The last imperial palace built for a Qing ruler is located in Changchun, the provincial capital of Jilin, north-east of Shenyang. It was here that Puyi was enthroned as the emperor of Manchukuo by the Japanese Imperial Army in

March 1934. His reign ended with the defeat of Japan in 1945, but his Western-style 'Puppet Imperial Palace' (*Wei Huang-gong*) and its forlorn garden is open to visitors.

THE TOMBS

Even the final resting places of the dead emperors and imperial ladies were regarded as part of the network of palaces. Ancestor worship required that rulers, or their representatives, make regular supplication at their forebears' tombs. In life emperors would often initiate the search for a 'propitious site for ten thousand years' (*wannian jidi*) shortly after ascending the throne, following which an underground crypt, called a 'subterranean palace' (*di gong*), and sumptuous sacrificial halls were built. The stunning location and vast scale of what are today called the Ming and Qing tombs give the visitor an idea of the afterlife which the emperors and their consorts expected to enjoy.

Especially noteworthy among the Ming tombs, which are north-west of Beijing, are Chang Ling, the truly imperial-scale tomb of the Yongle Emperor, during whose reign the Forbidden City was created in its present form, and Ding Ling, the excavated tomb of the Wanli Emperor, outside of which the exhumed corpse of the emperor and his two consorts were dressed in court robes, denounced at a mass rally and destroyed at the beginning of the Cultural Revolution. Ding Ling also boasts a site museum which houses objects salvaged from the excavation of the tomb.

The burial sites of the earliest Qing emperors, the Northern Tomb (*Bei Ling*) of the Tianming Emperor ('heavenly mandate', Nurhaci, r. 1616–25) and the Eastern Tomb (*Dong Ling*) of Chongde ('respect virtue', Hong Taiji, r. 1636–43), are located outside Shenyang. As for the tombs of emperors who ruled from the Forbidden City, the magnificent mausolea of the Shunzhi, Kangxi and Qianlong emperors can be seen at the Eastern Qing Tombs (*Qing Dong Ling*) in Zunhua county, Hebei province, 125 kilometres east of Beijing. Also located here are the paired tombs of the Empress Dowager Cixi (looted in 1928) and the Empress Dowager Ci'an, which are part of Ding Ling, the sepulchre of their imperial lord, the Xianfeng Emperor.

The Western Qing Tombs (*Qing Xi Ling*) are located in Yishui county, also in Hebei province, approximately 140 kilometres south-west of the capital. The tomb of the Yongzheng Emperor (*Tai Ling*) is on the grand scale of the high Qing, while the burial place of the Daoguang Emperor ('glory of right principle', r. 1821–50) called Mu Ling is a study in imperial restraint. As a prince the future emperor distinguished himself by helping fight off rebels of the Heavenly Principle religious sect who infiltrated the Forbidden City in 1813. However, the austere appearance of his tomb reflects the humiliation he felt for having subsequently mishandled the First Opium War in 1840–42. Here also the forlorn sepulchre of the Guangxu Emperor (*Chong Ling*) shows how far the wealth and style of the Great Qing had fallen by the end of their rule (the tomb was completed in the early years of the Republic of China which replaced the dynasty). The unadorned grave of the last emperor Puyi is located in the hills behind Guangxu's tomb, flanked by the (empty) tomb of his empress, Wanrong, and that of his last wife Li Shuxian. The visitor can stay at the Detached Palace Guesthouse (*Xinggong Binguan*) near the Eternal Fortune lama temple (*Yongfu Si*). The guesthouse was once a real detached palace where rulers like Qianlong and the Empress Dowager (who travelled there in 1903 by train) stayed when they came to offer sacrifice at the tombs.

FURTHER READING

Numerous Chinese and English sources have been consulted in the process of writing this volume. Footnotes and additional materials can be found online at <www.chinaheritageproject. org/theforbiddencity>. The following is a guide to major reference works and suggested reading.

INTRODUCTION

There are many books about the mystique of China, but a readable, and important, work is Jonathan D. Spence's *The Chan's Great Continent: China in Western Minds* (New York, 1998). For the myths and realities surrounding the other great Chinese icon, see Claire Roberts and Geremie R. Barmé, eds., *The Great Wall of China* (Sydney, 2006). The quotation about the Forbidden City is from Simon Leys (Pierre Ryckmans), *Chinese Shadows* (New York, 1977). Peter Quennell's *A Superficial Journey through Tokyo and Peking* (London, 1932; reissued Hong Kong and Oxford, 1986, with an introduction by Geremie Barmé), evokes the city of Beijing in the mid 1920s, as does George N. Kates's *The Years That Were Fat: The Last of Old China* (Cambridge, MA, 1967) for the 1930s and David Kidd's *Peking Story: The Last Days of Old China* (London, 1988) for the late 1940s. An example of the kind of contemporary cultural studies work on China being produced in the influential North American academy is Lydia H. Liu's *The Clash of Empires: The Invention of China in Modern World Making* (Cambridge, MA, 2004). The concluding chapter on the emperor's empty throne is of particular interest.

CHAPTER I: A PALACE OF BLOOD AND TEARS

For an atmospheric visual account of old Beijing, see Hedda Morrison, *A Photographer in Old Peking* (Hong Kong, 1985) and Osvald Sirén's *The Walls and Gates of Peking* (New York, 1924). Susan Naquin's *Peking: Temples and City Life, 1400–1900* (Berkeley, CA, 2000) offers a history of the city before its modern ruination, while Madeleine Yue Dong's *Republican Beijing: The City and Its Histories* (Berkeley, CA, 2003) is a useful work about the city in the pre-1949 era. Two powerful and heartfelt accounts of the destruction of the city under the Communists are Simon Leys' *Chinese Shadows*, mentioned above, and Tiziano Terzani's essay 'Death by a Thousand Cuts' in his *Behind the Forbidden Door* (London, 1985). Wang Jun's *Cheng Ji* (*An Account of the Walled City*) (Beijing, 2003) is one of the first popular descriptions of the 1950–70s destruction of old Beijing based on archival research. See also the website of the NGO Beijing Cultural Heritage Protection Center at <www.bjchp.org>.

The evolution of Beijing's urban design has been the focus of much recent writing in English. The art historian Wu Hung's *Remaking Beijing: Tiananmen Square and the Creation of a Political Space* (Chicago, 2005) provides a detailed and personal consideration of Communist-era Beijing. See also Victor F. S. Sit, *Beijing: The Nature and Planning of a Chinese*

Capital City (Chichester, 1995) and Wu Liangyong, *Rehabilitating the Old City of Beijing: A Project in the Ju'er Hutong Neighbourhood* (Vancouver, 1999). *Beijing Time* by Michael Dutton, Stacy Lo and Dong Dong Wu (Cambridge, MA, 2008) provides a rather breathless account of Beijing in the lead-up to the 2008 Olympics. A considerable body of nostalgic literature about old Beijing exists in Chinese, but only a sampling of this can be savoured in English. See Lin Yutang, *Imperial Peking: Seven Centuries of China* (London, 1961; reissued Ware, Herts., 1983). The documentary film *Morning Sun* (Boston, 2003), directed by Carma Hinton, Geremie R. Barmé and Richard Gordon, and its accompanying website, <www.morningsun.org>, provide a history of the Cultural Revolution and its culture, including material on *The Rent Collection Courtyard* (1965) and the 1964 song and dance epic *The East is Red*.

CHAPTER 2: THE ARCHITECTURE OF HIERARCHY

A good guide to the old city of Beijing and the Forbidden City is still the 1930s work by L. C. Arlington and William Lewisohn, *In Search of Old Peking* (Peking, 1935; reissued with an introduction by Geremie Barmé, Oxford and Hong Kong, 1987), although Graeme Smith's *Frommer's Beijing* (Hoboken, NJ, 2006) is an excellent and amusing introduction to contemporary Beijing. Susan Naquin's *Peking: Temples and City Life, 1400–1900*, mentioned above, is the best overall study of the city through its history. Shih-Shan Henry Tsai's *Perpetual Happiness: The Ming Emperor Yongle* (Seattle, 2001) gives an account of the Ming founder of modern Beijing and builder of the Forbidden City. The palace itself is well described by Yu

Zhuoyun in *Palaces of the Forbidden City* (London and New York, 1984), May Holdsworth in *The Forbidden City* (Oxford, 1998) and by Shan Shiyuan in *The Story of the Imperial Palace and Its Buildings* (Beijing, 2005). A convenient small guide is *The Forbidden City: Center of Imperial China* by Gilles Béguin and Dominique Motel (New York, 1997). A standard Chinese reference work is Wan Yi, ed., *Gugong Cidian* (*Dictionary of the Former Palace*) (Shanghai, 1996), while useful Qing-era accounts are E'ertai and Zhang Tingyu's *Guochao Gongshi* (*A History of the Dynastic Palaces*) (Beijing, 1987) and Qinggui's *Guochao Gongshi Xubian* (*A Supplementary History of the Dynastic Palaces*) (Beijing, 1994). A useful work on the palace and Qing emperors is Musée du Petit Palais, *La Cité interdite: Vie publique et privée des empereurs de Chine (1644–1911)* (Paris, 1996). Ray Huang's *1587: A Year of No Significance: The Ming Dynasty in Decline* (New Haven, CT., 1981) is an evocative account of the Forbidden City and the activities of the late Ming Wanli Emperor, while Taisuke Mitamura's *Chinese Eunuchs: The Structure of Intimate Politics*, Charles A. Pomeroy, trans. (Boston, 1970) remains an important study of the rise of eunuchs in Chinese court politics. F. W. Mote's *Imperial China: 900–1800* (Cambridge, MA, 1999) provides a meticulous history of the Ming and early Qing eras.

Many studies examining the design and architecture of the Forbidden City and specific buildings within it have appeared in *Gugong Bowuyuan Yuankan* (Palace Museum Journal), now published as a bimonthly; *Zijin Cheng* (Forbidden City), a journal that began publication in 1980; and *Gugong Xuekan* (Journal of Former Palace Studies), an annual collection of scholarly papers that first appeared in 2004. A definitive work on the geomantic principles employed in the construction of the Forbidden City is Wang Zilin's *Zijin Cheng Fengshui* (*The* Fengshui *of the Forbidden City*) (Beijing, 2005). See also Nancy Shatzman Steinhardt's *Chinese Imperial City Planning* (Honolulu, 1990). A colourful account of various early foreign encounters with the Forbidden City can be found in Maurice Collis' *The Great Within* (London, 1941).

CHAPTER 3: RISE AND DECLINE

Ann Paludan's *Chronicle of the Chinese Emperors: The Reign-by-Reign Record of the Rulers of Imperial China* (London, 1998) offers a useful guide to reigns, titles and the history of imperial rule, while Pamela Kyle Crossley's *The Manchus* (Cambridge, MA, and Oxford, 1997) is an excellent study of the evolution of the Manchus and the manner in which they and their Mongolian and Han allies ruled China as the Great Qing. Evelyn S. Rawski, *The Last Emperors, A Social History of Qing Imperial Institutions* (Berkeley, CA, 1998), is an authoritative guide to late imperial Chinese dynastic practice. Peter C. Perdue's *China Marches West: The Qing Conquest of Central Asia* (Cambridge, MA and London, 2005) follows the history of the expansion of the multi-ethnic Qing empire under the three emperors.

The 'three emperors' have been the subject of a number of major studies, and there are many first-hand accounts of meetings and audiences with Kangxi and Qianlong written by Chinese contemporaries. Their lives and personalities (or rather 'presences') were also assiduously documented by the Europeans with whom they came into contact. An excellent starting point for further reading in English on the period is Evelyn S. Rawski and Jessica Rawson, eds., *China: The Three*

Emperors 1662–1795 (London, 2006). A detailed 'tour' of four of the scroll paintings made of Kangxi and Qianlong's southern tours can be seen at <www.mcah.columbia.edu/nanxuntu/start.html>. There is a considerable corpus of work on the contributions of the Jesuits to the Ming and Qing courts in Chinese and European languages, but Kangxi's candid comments and impressions of these Jesuit visitors and would-be advisers are contained in Jonathan D. Spence's *Emperor of China: Self-portrait of K'ang-hsi* (New York, 1974). Spence's study of the Yongzheng Emperor, *Treason by the Book* (New York, 2001), is also an important work on this still little-appreciated ruler, while A. E. Grantham's *A Manchu Monarch: An Interpretation of Chia Ch'ing* (London, 1934), gives an account of the Qing court in its early decline, as well as of the 1813 invasion of the Forbidden City by a group of rebels aided by disaffected eunuchs. See Cao Xueqin, *The Story of the Stone: A Chinese Novel in Five Volumes* (Harmondsworth, 1973–86), translated by David Hawkes (vols. 1–3) and John Minford (the volumes by Cao Xueqin and Gao E, vols. 4–5), for the most famous novel depicting the life of splendour in mid eighteenth-century China. Joanna Waley-Cohen's *The Sextants of Beijing: Global Currents in Chinese History* (New York and London, 1999) offers insights into the ways in which dynastic China was constantly changing, engaging with major trends and adapting to them, with varying degrees of success.

CHAPTER 4: A DAY IN THE REIGN

This chapter is largely based on Wu Shizhou's *Qianlong Yiri* (*One Day in the Life of Qianlong*) (Jinan, 2006). There are few English language studies of the Qianlong Emperor, and the problems facing any biographer are ably discussed in Harold L. Kahn's insightful *Monarchy in the Emperor's Eyes: Image and Reality in the Ch'ien-lung Reign* (Cambridge, MA, 1971). An important work is Pamela Kyle Crossley's *A Translucent Mirror: History and Identity in Qing Imperial Ideology* (Berkeley, CA, 1999), while a standard contemporary assessment of the Qianlong Emperor and his position in history is Bai Xinliang's *Qianlong Huangdi Zhuan* (*Biography of the Qianlong Emperor*) (Tianjin, 2004). An introduction to the poetry of Qianlong is Sun Piren and Bu Weiyi, eds., *Qianlong Shi Xuan* (*Selected Poems of Qianlong*) (Shenyang, 1987). The translated excerpt of Wang Xizhi's fourth-century 'Preface to the Orchid Pavilion Poems' is by H. C. Chang, collected in the extraordinary *Classical Chinese Literature: An Anthology of Translations, Vol. 1: From Antiquity to the Tang Dynasty*, John Minford and Joseph S. M. Lau, eds. (New York and Hong Kong, 2000).

CHAPTER 5: THE DOWAGER

See J. O. P. Bland and E. Backhouse, *China under the Empress Dowager: Being the History of the Life and Times of Tzu-Hsi, compiled from State Papers and the Private Diary of the Comptroller of Her Household* (London, 1905; reissued Whitefish, MT, 2007), and Sterling Seagrave's corrective, *Dragon Lady: The Life and Legend of the Last Empress of China*, with the collaboration of Peggy Seagrave (New York and London, 1992). Hugh Trevor-Roper's *Hermit of Peking: The Hidden Life of Sir Edmund Backhouse* (Harmondsworth, 1978) offers a furious account of Backhouse's extraordinary life and Cyril Pearl's *Morrison of Peking* (Sydney and London, 1967) is still worth consulting, although for a detailed debunking of the Jingshan myth it is essential to read the meticulous analysis by the Morrison expert Lo Hui-min, 'The Ching-shan Diary: A Clue to Its Forgery', *East Asian History*, No. 1 (June 1991), pp. 98–124. See also Victor Segalen's *René Leys*, J. A. Underwood, trans. (New York, 1998; reissued with a preface by Ian Buruma, 2003), and Sir Edmund Trelawny Backhouse, *Décadence Manchoue* (Peking, 1943; unpublished manuscript). *The Tiananmen Papers*, compiled by Zhang Liang and edited by Andrew J. Nathan and Perry Link, with an afterword by Orville Schell (New York, 2001), is a recent work in the tradition of Backhousean historiography. Yu Der Ling's *Two Years in the Forbidden City* (New York, 1911) and Katherine Augusta Carl's *With the Empress Dowager of China* (New York, 1907; reissued Whitefish, MT, 2004) give detailed descriptions of the Empress Dowager's court in her last years. Shortly before the return of Hong Kong to China in 1997, the Palace Museum supported a rare exhibition of artefacts related to the Empress Dowager as a gesture of goodwill to the former British colony. See the catalogue edited by Wang Baoguang, et al., *Empress Dowager Cixi: Her Art of Living* (Hong Kong, 1996). For more on the women in the imperial seraglio, see Wilt Idema and Beata Grant, eds., *The Red Brush: Writing Women of Imperial China* (Cambridge, MA, 2004) and May Holdsworth, *Adorning the Empress* (Hong Kong, 2006).

A discussion of the complex echoes of patriotism in relation to the Manchu court and the decline of the Qing dynasty can be found in the issue of *China Heritage Quarterly* devoted to the Garden of Perfect Brightness (<www.chinaheritagequarterly.org>, issue 8, December 2006) and see also the chapter 'To Screw Foreigners is Patriotic' in my *In the Red: On Contemporary Chinese Culture* (New York, 1999). *55 Days at Peking* was directed by Nicholas Ray and released by Allied Artists in 1963. An overview account of the events of 1900 is Peter Fleming's *The Siege at Peking* (London, 1959; reissued, Oxford, 1984), while Jane E. Elliot's *Some Did It for Civilisation, Some Did It for Their Country: A Revised View of the Boxer War* (Hong Kong, 2002) offers an insightful analysis of the foreign reporting on China in the nineteenth and early twentieth centuries, and its long-term impact. Paul A. Cohen's *History in Three Keys: The Boxers as Event, Experience, and Myth* (New York, 1997) provides a nuanced study of the rebellion and its historical resonances.

CHAPTER 6: WITHIN AND WITHOUT THE PALACE

For details of Puyi's reign and later life, see Reginald Fleming Johnston, *Twilight in the Forbidden City* (London, 1934) and Aisin-Gioro Pu Yi, *From Emperor to Citizen – The Autobiography of Aisin-Gioro Pu Yi*, 2 vols., W. J. F. Jenner, trans. (Oxford, 1997). Chang Lin-sheng's 'The National Palace Museum: A History of the Collection' in Wen C. Fong and James C. Y. Watt, eds., *Possessing the Past: Treasures from the National Palace Museum, Taipei* (New York, 1996) is the most readily accessible account of the museum. Another is the error-ridden *The Odyssey of China's Imperial Art Treasures* (Seattle, 2005) by Jeannette Shambaugh Elliott, with David Shambaugh, which gives an outline of the Palace Museum's evolution in the eras of the Republic and People's Republic. Claire Roberts discusses some of the ironies surrounding the Yi Peiji case in 'Questions of Authenticity: Huang Binhong and the Palace Museum', *China Heritage Quarterly* (<www.

chinaheritagequarterly.org>), issue 10 (March 2007), under 'New Scholarship'. Cheng-hua Wang's 'The Qing Imperial Collection, Circa 1905–25: National Humiliation, Heritage Preservation, and Exhibition Culture' (forthcoming) is an important source, and details of some of the other material consulted for this chapter can be found in *China Heritage Quarterly*, issue 4 (December 2005), which is devoted to the eightieth anniversary of the Palace Museum. The websites of the Palace Museums in Beijing and Taipei are also worth visiting at <www.dpm.org.cn/English/default.asp> and <www.npm.gov.tw/en/home.htm> respectively.

CHAPTER 7: THREE HUNDRED YEARS ON

Accessible modern histories include Jonathan D. Spence's *The Search for Modern China* (New York, 1990) and *The Gate of Heavenly Peace: The Chinese and their Revolution, 1895–1980* (New York, 1981) as well as Immanuel C.Y. Hsu, *The Rise of Modern China* (Oxford, 1970). For details of Manchuria, see Lucien Gibert, *Dictionnaire historique et géographique de la Mandchourie* (Hong Kong, 1934). On the entry of the Manchus to Beijing through the Great Wall, see my chapter 'Prince Gong's Folly' in Roberts and Barmé, *The Great Wall of China*, mentioned above. Guo Moruo's lengthy essay, 'Commemoration of the Three-Hundredth Year since *Jiashen* [1644]' was published as a booklet, *Jiashen Sanbainian Ji*, in Beijing in 1972 (latest impression, 2004). For countless numbers of Chinese readers, the history of the fall of the Ming and the early rule of the Qing is 'studied' by reading popular kung-fu fiction by bestselling authors such as Louis Cha (Jin Yong). See, for example, his *Lu Ding Ji* masterfully translated in three volumes as *The Deer & the Cauldron* by John Minford (Hong Kong and New York, 2000–2003), which contains numerous scenes set in the Forbidden City. Henrietta Harrison's *The Making of the Republican Citizen: Political Ceremonies and Symbols in China, 1911–1929* (Oxford and New York, 2000) covers the crucial early years of the Chinese Republic. An authoritative resource on the Lake Palaces is Zhongguo Diyi Lishi Dang'anguan, ed., *Qingdai Zhongnan Hai Dang'an* (*Qing Dynasty Zhongnan Hai Archive*) (Beijing, 2004), 30 volumes. A more accessible account is Wu Kong's *Zhongnan Hai Shiji* (*Historical Traces in the Lake Palaces*) (Beijing, 1998). A description of the Lake Palaces during the Mao era is given by Li Zhisui in his *The Private Life of Chairman Mao: The Memoirs of Mao's Personal Physician Dr Li Zhisui*, trans. Tai Hung-chao with Anne F. Thurston (New York, 1994), while Richard Curt Kraus's *Brushes with Power: Modern Politics and the Chinese Art of Calligraphy* (Berkeley, CA, 1991) is an excellent study of how the arts of calligraphy and politics remained enmeshed in Chinese life well into the twentieth century. For an account of the 1989 protest movement and its historical context, see the film *The Gate of Heavenly Peace* (Boston, 1995), directed by Carma Hinton and Richard Gordon, and written by Geremie Barmé with John Crowley, and the accompanying website <www.tsquare.tv>.

CHAPTER 8: THE BANQUET OF HISTORY

Alain Peyrefitte, *The Collision of Two Civilizations: The British Expedition to China in 1792–4*, trans. Jon Rothschild (London, 1993) and James L. Hevia, *Cherishing Men from Afar: Qing Guest Ritual and the Macartney Embassy of 1793* (Durham,

NC, and London, 1995) provide contrasting accounts of the famous encounter between high Qing China and the mercantile empire of George III's Britain. James L. Hevia's *English Lessons: The Pedagogy of Imperialism in Nineteenth-century China* (Durham, NC, 2003) is also interesting in this context. Ye Xiaoqing, 'Ascendant Peace in the Four Seas: Tributary Drama and the Macartney Mission of 1793' in *Late Imperial China*, vol. 26, no. 2 (December 2005) is a study of the drama staged for Macartney and his mission, and the source of the opera quoted here. Margaret MacMillan's *Nixon and Mao: The Week That Changed the World* (New York, 2007) is a recent readable account of the encounter between the leaders of China and the US. The Qing historian Susan Naquin offers a meticulous overview of how the Palace Museum exhibits itself internationally in 'The Forbidden City Goes Abroad: Qing History and the Foreign Exhibitions of the Palace Museum, 1974–2004', *T'oung Pao*, vol. 90 (2004) (Fascicle 4–5), pp. 341–97, which has been used in this chapter. For a comment on the spectacle of the 2008 Beijing Olympics and Zhang Yimou's involvement, see my essay 'Let the Spiel Begin', an online version of which was posted on 24 July 2006 at <www.danwei.org/2008_beijing_olympic_games/let_the_spiel_begin_by_geremie.php>. The concluding poem 'Cauldron' (*Ding*) (1996) by Leung Ping-kwan was translated by John Minford and Chan Oi-sum.

LIST OF ILLUSTRATIONS

ILLUSTRATION CREDITS

8, 10, 18, 19, 23, 25, 26 author's photograph; 12, 14, 15
Palace Museum; 20 Macau: First Town Company; 22
George E. Morrison Papers, Mitchell Library, State Library
of New South Wales, Sydney; 32 Guilin: Guangxi Shifan
Daxue Chubanshe; 33 Powerhouse Museum, Sydney.

ACKNOWLEDGEMENTS

It is a quarter of a century since members of the Central Guard Bureau detained me in the Lake Palaces. I had entered the scenic headquarters of the Chinese Communist Party, along with numerous Chinese tourists, to see Mao's old residence at the Garden of Abundant Nourishment and to visit the Ocean Terrace. Although I had a legitimate entry ticket that allowed me access through the West Garden Gate, I did not realise that, as has so often been the case when trying to visit the more recondite sights of Beijing, foreigners were not welcome. I still feel a pang of guilt for this unintentional mischief as it resulted in a Central Committee Office investigation into all of my friends and contacts in the city. Previous and subsequent visits to the rest of the 'Great Within' were never quite so dramatic.

This book was written with the support of an Australian Research Council Federation Fellowship which has allowed me to pursue my work on Beijing as a city of spectacle from 1710 to 2010. As ever, The Australian National University has provided me with the conditions and freedom to read, write, travel and interact with a unique body of scholars.

I am particularly grateful to Sang Ye, long-term collaborator and friend, for the crucial contributions he has made to this book. I have relied heavily on his encyclopaedic knowledge of Beijing, both old and new, and he has been unstinting in providing crucial material on and insights into the post-1949 history of the Forbidden City.

Bruce Doar, who embarked on this project with me, made major contributions to the drafting of the chapters related to the dynastic history of the Forbidden City (chapters 2, 3 and 4), as well as the chapter on the transformation of the Forbidden City into the Palace Museum in the twentieth century (chapter 6).

Linda Jaivin, novelist, translator and editor extraordinaire, read the full draft of the book and made numerous suggestions on style, content and voice which were crucial as I turned the wordy and academic original into something that I hope non-specialist readers can enjoy. My close friend John Minford was kind enough to read through the manuscript with great care twice and his numerous suggestions have helped eliminate stylistic inconsistencies and add greater colour to the dynastic palace. He also revised the poem on the heads of the Khojas, Elder and Younger, that appears at the beginning of chapter 2 and suggested ways to extend the material related to the Yongzheng Emperor. Other readers of the full manuscript or of individual chapters are Margaret Jolly (who encouraged me to add 'A Reader's Guide'), Gloria Davies and Claire Roberts, all of whom have offered useful suggestions. Adam Driver shared insights into the mind of E. T. Backhouse. Oanh Collins and Jenny Sackl of the Division of Pacific and Asian History in the Research School of Pacific and Asian Studies at The Australian National University scanned images for me and my film-maker colleagues Nora Chang and Richard Gordon were generous in helping me locate illustrations in the Long Bow Archive in Boston.

Claire Roberts brought the work of the No Name artists and Chen Danqing to my attention and Jeremy Clarke, SJ, provided information on the Empress Dowager-inspired Chinese Catholic portrayal of Mary, Mother of Jesus.

I am particularly grateful to my friend Jeffrey N. Wasserstrom for encouraging me to pursue this project and for introducing me to the editor of 'Wonders of the World', Mary Beard, who offered many insightful comments that helped me revise the final draft. The publisher Peter Carson was enthusiastic about this book from its inception, not least of all because it touches on a fascinating episode in his family history (see page 160). My editor at Profile Books, Nicola Taplin, has been patient and encouraging at all the crucial moments, and my copy editor Sally Holloway was punctilious and demanding in her careful revision of the text. The cover design by Stuart Brill is also one that resonates well with the book's complex content.

This book is dedicated to Jocelyn Chey and to the memory of Hans Moon Lin Chey, friends and mentors from my earliest days in China.

INDEX

G

WONDERS OF THE WORLD

This is a small series of books, under the general editorship of Mary Beard, that will focus on some of the world's most famous sites or monuments.